Professionals Praise *Every Page Perfect*

• • •

"What every professional writer should know—and most of [illegible]on't."
• **Tony Hillerman**, Author

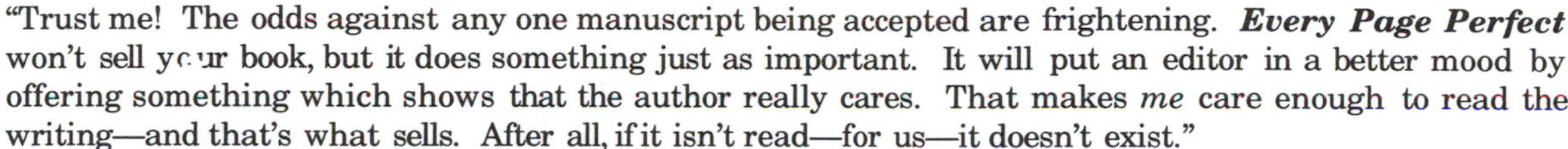

"Trust me! The odds against any one manuscript being accepted are frightening. ***Every Page Perfect*** won't sell your book, but it does something just as important. It will put an editor in a better mood by offering something which shows that the author really cares. That makes *me* care enough to read the writing—and that's what sells. After all, if it isn't read—for us—it doesn't exist."
• **Michael Seidman**, Editor, Walker & Co.

"The only manuscript format guide a writer will ever need."
• **Sharon Jarvis**, Literary Agent, Publisher, Toad Hall Press

"The easiest way *not* to sell a book is to present it to an editor in an unprofessional fashion. ***Every Page Perfect*** shows how to present work in a very professional manner. While this doesn't guarantee you're going to sell your book, it sure puts you way ahead of the game. If you have talent, you'll sell. But a professional-quality presentation will get editors to read your book ahead of the unprofessional work that equally talented writers submit to them.
• **James Frenkel**, Publisher, Bluejay Books

"Where was ***Every Page Perfect*** when I was getting started?! Writers may reach the best-seller status without reading ***Every Page Perfect***, but the path to success will certainly be shorter and easier if they do."
• **Paris Bonds**, Author

"A responsible parent wouldn't think of sending a teenager off to a job interview without a clean shirt and polished shoes; a responsible writer wouldn't think of sending a query or manuscript off to a publisher without ***Every Page Perfect***. Here's a book that will help any writer get the job done right!
• **Lois Duncan**, Author

" . . . right on target . . . "
• **Jean Fredette**, Editor, Writer's Digest Books

"***Every Page Perfect*** is filled with sound, practical, and essential information and advice for every writer."
• **Jack Bickham**, Author, Professor of Professional Writing Emeritus

"***{Every Page Perfect}*** does for manuscript submissions what Miss Manners did for daily etiquette—reveal to everyone what is expected and how to behave in order to achieve what you desire—get published!"
• **Diane C. Donovan**, Editor, *The Midwest Book Review*

"Don't go near your typewriter without it!"
• **Madge Harrah**, Author, Playwright, Songwriter, Poet, Musician

"Writers who have respect for their own work must have this book."
• **Norman Zollinger**, Author

"Timely, informative, and authoritative. Belongs on every writer's and would-be writer's desk."
• **William J. Buchanan**, Author, Teacher

"***Every Page Perfect*** contains everything I need to prepare a correct manuscript."
• **Delorez Roupe**, Writer

"This book is going on my reference shelf; I highly recommend it."
• **Debbie Ridpath Ohi**, Editor, Inklings, on-line newsletter for writers

"For professional writers, this is one of the most inclusive guides on preparing and submitting manuscripts available."
• ***The Oklahoman***

Professionals Praise *Every Page Perfect*

• • •

"Another good book for your reference shelf . . . Never again will you have a ms rejected because it was on the wrong paper or had too skinny a margin. Includes sample letters and full-sized models to give you a clear picture of what editors and publishers want, for just about every genre imaginable."

• ***Writing for Money***

"Maybe you can't tell a good book by its cover, but you can certainly tell a lot about a writer from a manuscript. ***Every Page Perfect*** shows you how to put your best foot forward. The rest of the walk is up to your writing."

• **Jim Morris**, Editor, Dell Books

"I want every writer to buy a copy of ***Every Page Perfect***, and I'm sending out a flyer about this book with every unprofessional-looking manuscript I return."

• **Happy Shaw**, Literary Agent, Remington Literary Agency

"There is no substitute for ***Every Page Perfect***! In some forty years of writing for a living, I've seen them all, and there's never been a book on manuscript formatting and submission protocol that I've found more constructive, more useful, or more absolutely necessary."

• **Eileen Stanton**, Author, Teacher, TV & Radio Producer

"Valuable because it advises the writer of the distinction that must be made in addressing the editors and publishers of different categories of the printed word. Nonfiction or fiction, short or long—each requires a different approach, and this book provides samples and explanations of each."

• **Joann Mazzio**, Author

"You can search a hundred books for this information, or you can save yourself lots of time, money, rejection, heartache, and frustration by buying ***Every Page Perfect*** the first time around."

• **Kathryn Fanning**, Managing Editor, *ByLine Magazine*

"This book is great for the novice writer and I heartily recommend it."

• **Yvonne MacManus**, author of *You Can Write a Romance and Get It Published.*

"With this book, there is no reason why any manuscript you submit is not in proper form. I highly recommend you purchase this one."

• **Elizabeth Klungness**, Editor, *Writer's News*

"This book contains everything you need to know about form . . . Nothing is left out . . . and since it is full 8 1/2 by 11 inches in size, you see the layout actual size."

• **Carrillee Collins**, Editor, *Yesterday's Magazette*

"It ***[Every Page Perfect]*** does, indeed, offer full size examples of how to prepare the proper format for everything a writer might send out—"

• ***Writers International Forum***

"***[Every Page Perfect]*** even covers the 'dreaded' synopsis, a requirement that causes even the most proficient writer to cringe."

• **Jeannine D. Van Eperen**, Editor, *LERA Lyrics*

"If, as a beginner who hasn't already learned manuscript preparation, you don't feel that acquiring this book is the most interesting and important thing you can do this week, then you shouldn't bother to try to sell your fiction or nonfiction to the publishing industry.

• **Jacqueline Lichtenberg**, Reviewer, *The Monthly Aspectarian*

"A guide to the entire process from idea to completed professional-looking submission, from query letter to manuscript."

• **Outdoor Writers Association of America, Inc**

"Highly recommended as a basic guide with clearly written advice."

• **Linda Hutton**, Publisher, Hutton Publications

• • •

EVERY PAGE PERFECT

• • •

A Full-Size Writer's Manual for *Manuscript Format* & *Submission Protocol*

The First and Still The *Only* Full-Size Writer's Guide to Manuscripts That $ell!

Lynnx Ink • 4th Edition
Revised and Updated
Glossary & Index

by

Mary Lynn

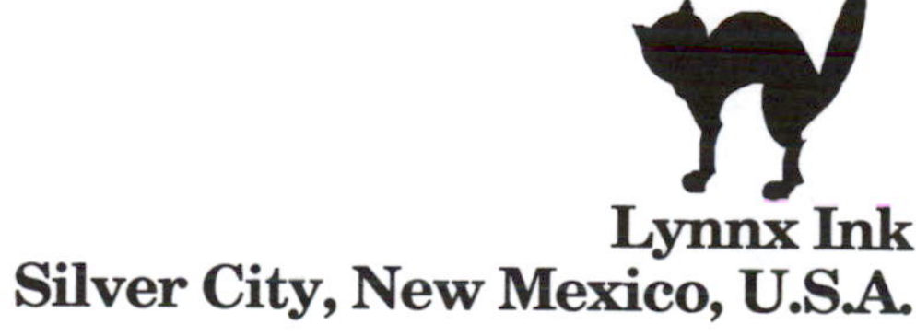

Lynnx Ink
Silver City, New Mexico, U.S.A.

EVERY PAGE PERFECT
A Full-Size Writer's Manual for Manuscript Format & Submission Protocol
by Mary Lynn

ISBN 0-9710143-0-2

CompuPress/Sandia Publishing History:
First edition: August 1987

Lynnx Ink Publishing History:
Second edition: January 1995

Toad Hall Press Publishing History:
Third edition: January 1997

Lynnx Ink Publishing History:
Fourth edition: May 2001

Lynnx Ink
6 Burke Loop
Silver City, New Mexico 88061
U.S.A.

Printed in the United States of America

Dedication

• • •

To Ted, the partner who found a way—

•

To Jack Bickham, the friend who showed the way—

•

To Terri, Jon, Kim, and Chris, who know the way—

•

To Darryl and Dan, who delight the way.

• • •

• ACKNOWLEDGMENTS •

A Special Thanks to—

EDITORS: Michael Seidman, Pat LoBrutto, Leslie Wainger, Isabel Swift, Tara Gavin, Melissa Ann Singer, Debra Matteucci, Jean Fredette, Karen Solem, Jim Morris, Kathryn Fanning, Marcia Preston, Brooke Comer, Jennifer Hershey, Geri Mosher, Lois Hazel, Abigail Kamen Holland, Sheila Cavanagh, Greg Aaron, Julianne Moore.

WRITERS: Jack Bickham, Dwight Swain, Marilyn Lill, Judy Wall, Judy Murphy, Kathy Kunz, Lois Duncan, Kathy Marcouiller, Tony Hillerman, William Buchanan, Ted Lynn, Delorez Roupe, Norman Zollinger, Eileen Stanton, Don Stanton, Jerry Weber, Madge Harrah, Paula Paul, Donald Westlake, Clive Cussler, Jean Hager, Carolyn Hart, Judy Steel, Kay Lewis 'Happy' Shaw, Rosemary Clemiato, Kathy Hull Edwards, Guy Ashley Edwards, Jene Moseley, Joann Mazzio, Paris Bonds, Jheri Fleet, Georgia McKinney, Suzanne Spletzer, Sara Probasco, Rick Reichman, Chris Vogler, Ann Rule, Mary Higgins Clark, Sue Grafton, Elsie Kreischer, Linda Galloway, Susan Heiman (bookseller and friend to all writers), Sarah Lovett, Pam Hendrickson, Maria Price, Joyce Corral, Lynn Cartland, Ginger & Lou Ollivier, Carla DeMarco, Lucielle South, Ann Elliott, Helen & Barney Himes, Jessie Ruebush, Susie Jerome, Larry Martin & Linda Locklar-Martin, Steve Healy, Steve Bennett, J. Lynn Cutts, June E. Gibb, Jo Ann Hamlin, Sue Mann, Scot Pearson, George Bayless, Stephan Gladish, Christina Garcia, Lois Webb, and Nancy Taylor Rosenberg (for table-sharing). {This list is quasi-complete because of space limitations.}

AGENTS: Dixie Lee Davidson, Anita Diamant, Sharon Jarvis, Elizabeth Cavanaugh, Pat LoBrutto, Meredith Bernstein, Ricia Mainhardt, Kay Lewis 'Happy' Shaw, A. Phyllis Pinzow, Peter Miller, Jennifer Robinson, Jeff Herman, Barbara Gislason.

PUBLISHERS: James Frenkel, Tom McCormack, Tom Doherty, Stan DeGeer, Harry Willson, Diane Duff, and Dutch Salmon.

For EDITING & PROOFING: Kimberli Ann Wilson, A. Phyllis Pinzow, Yvonne MacManus, and Margaret Carter

For PROOFING, ABOVE & BEYOND: June E. Gibb

For INVALUABLE ADVICE: My writing students

For CREATIVE ASSISTANCE:
Black One, Nutter One, Sugar, Mama Cass, Baby Cass, Patches, Daily Dog, Babbit, Robber Cass, Tiger Dude, Macho, Taajah, Kelpie, Dancer, Tzarita, Separ, Tzarik, Fiannah, Troubles, CC, Critter, Flash, Zeus, PK, and the thirteen Pepés-le-Fuse.

Also thanks to all my writing students and all SouthWest Writers members! They've taught me much more than I've ever taught them.

• Contents •

• • •

Poetry and Verse - *Continued*

• • •

Book-Length Fiction - *Continued*

• • •

• • •

• FOREWORD •

(To the first edition)

by

Dwight V. Swain

Back in the dark ages I received a doubtful compliment from an editor who bought a lot of stories from me.

"Swain," he said, "your stories may not always be so hot. But if I'm in a hurry, all I have to do to them is mark the initials and send them to the printer."

That's hardly the kind of encomium you like to hear from someone who's judging your work. Yet as the years went by, I came to wonder if it didn't have its points. Because while he might be running down my literary genius, Editor *was* acknowledging that I knew how to put a story on paper.

Is that important? I think it is, as witness my experience with one writer some years later when I myself was editing copy.

This man's name was Ed Churchill. He worked as a publicity rep for Paramount Pictures, but his passion was small planes and he frequently contributed free-lance pieces to *Flying* Magazine, where I labored.

The arrival of an Ed Churchill article on my desk was a cause for celebration. The reason? Because it was so beautifully prepared as virtually to constitute an afternoon off for me. Never was a word misspelled, a comma misplaced, or a sentence scrambled. Format was ever and always perfect.

Contrast these with the messy, sloppy, poorly presented, amateurish efforts that too often came in over the transom. They didn't even *look* good. And I knew in advance that if I should happen to find some gem I had to buy for its content regardless of appearances, I was in for an hour or two of grueling concentration to bring it to minimal standards.

So whose manuscript gets rejected if it surfaces in late afternoon, with content that was only of so-so importance/interest?

Unfair? Of course. But also human.

—And not *too* unfair, at that. Because experience soon taught me that if a piece showed no awareness of editorial requirements, quite possibly it was also weak on accuracy and development.

The years haven't changed my reaction on these matters too much. Knowledge of editorial rules and format still rates as important—and not just with me. Only the other day, regional film producer/director Christopher Lewis commented to me, "The writers whose scripts I see haven't all learned format. They think all there is to it is just to get the idea down. To me, fundamentals are very important. If it says FADE OUT, you should know where to put it, and what to capitalize, and all that stuff. It makes it easier for the production manager to break it down."

It's experiences and comments like these that make me feel that *Every Page Perfect* is a catalogue of formats well-nigh as vital for a writer, professional or would-be, as a dictionary; and I hereby put myself on record as thanking the two young ladies who first prepared it. For even if you know format to within a gnat's eyebrow in one specialty, it's entirely possible to fall flat on embarrassing portions of your anatomy in others.

Which is why this is an ever-so-important book to add to your shelf—day before yesterday at the latest!

Dwight V. Swain

Dwight V. Swain wrote more than a million words of fact and fiction for magazines and over fifty films. He was a Professor of Professional Writing at the University of Oklahoma's School of Journalism and wrote several highly acclaimed books including *Techniques of the Selling Writer, Film Scriptwriting,* and *Scripting For Video and Audiovisual Media*. He was a member of the American Medical Writers Association, the Science Fiction Writers of America, and the University Film Association.

• INTRODUCTION •

• • •

If you go to a job interview wearing a pressed suit and shined shoes, you're likely to get at least a polite hearing, even if you're totally unqualified for the position. First impressions *do* matter and they *do* last.

Your manuscript submission is all the job interview you're likely to get as a freelance writer. From the moment your pages are removed from the envelope or manuscript box, your work must make the best impression possible. You want the editor to give your efforts a professional reading. To get one, your submission must look professional.

Seem superficial? Too simple? Doesn't everybody know better than to submit manuscripts on electric yellow, oddly-shaped pages that have been sprayed with Chanel #5?

Then why does almost every book on writing spend at least a page or two on manuscript preparation? Why do so many editors so often stand up at writers' conferences to beg for generous margins, good-quality paper, black ink, and readable type?

For the simple reason that editors have to read hundreds—even thousands—of manuscripts from the slush pile every year. Editors have to say "no" much more often than they can say "yes." A poorly prepared manuscript gives the editor the perfect excuse to hand down a rejection.

Don't let it happen to you!

That's the purpose of *Every Page Perfect.* Whether you write novels, articles, short stories, greeting cards—or anything else every serious freelancer is interested in selling—you'll find the proper format and submission process in *Every Page Perfect.*

Every Page Perfect was the first book to present the complete range of manuscript formats and submission protocol. A revised second edition included double the information and instruction. Query letters, partials, series proposals, book-length submissions, short stories, articles, poetry, verse, greeting cards, cover letters, news releases—in this completely new and revised edition—are all explained here, and much more, with dozens of examples. Every sample page appears full size and accurately spaced, looking just as your finished pages should.

And speaking of samples: Please note that throughout this book I've numbered the pages at the bottom of each body page so that the reader may find information easily. When submitting to publishers, however, use your own appropriate numbering at the top right corner of the manuscript page, as shown in the examples.

Now, whether your writing holds up under the scrutiny of an editor's eagle eye and his or her individual taste is another question. But by following the formats in *Every Page Perfect,* you'll have the best possible chance of catching the editor's attention. First impressions, remember? Whatever the form, whatever the submission, it's still a job interview just as surely as if you were sitting across the desk from a personnel manager.

On the subject of writing: In several parts of this book, I refer to plotting, characterization, and several other techniques I teach in my writing courses. For more information on these classes and workshops, send a letter, with SASE (self-addressed, stamped envelope), requesting information on both fiction and nonfiction sessions available. Write to: Lynnx Ink Workshops, 6 Burke Loop, Silver City, New Mexico 88061. E-mail: <mary@writerscenter.com>. Call: 505-388-3813, Monday through Friday, 10 AM to 4 PM MST. Contact via: <www.writerscenter.com>

Whatever your writing skill, level of expertise, or stage of progress, just remember these three little words: Never Give Up!

If your writing's good and you adhere to all of the professional standards set forth herein, all who read this book will eventually see their work in print. *You* must learn how to make your writing exciting. This manual will show you how to make ***Every Page Perfect!***

• • •

NOTE: Several style manuals have been consulted in the writing of *Every Page Perfect. The Chicago Manual of Style*, 14th Edition, has prevailed in most situations (especially in noting numbers), the following were also considered: *The Elements of Style* by William Strunk Jr. and E.B. White, *Words into Type*, *The Associated Press Stylebook and Libel Manual, The Word*, and *The Picture*.

REMINDER: Write for information about **Lynnx Ink Fact & Fiction Workshops** to: Lynnx Ink, 6 Burke Loop, Silver City NM 88061. E-mail: <mary@writerscenter.com>. Call us Monday through Friday, 10 AM to 4 PM MST, 505-388-3813. You may also contact us at <www.writerscenter.com> Lynnx Ink Workshops are conducted by special invitation only. Schools, colleges, universities, conferences, and writers' groups may contact Lynnx Ink for more info and/or for scheduling classes for one-, two-, or three-day workshops on the craft and business of writing. Workshop information is available year-round. •

A Chronology (of sorts): Proofreaders' Marks

In the course of doing business as a writer, you may expect to go through several stages of the editing process. For instance, after a writer finishes rewrites and revisions on a contracted book, the editor does the mechanical or line edit, which corrects problems of grammar, spelling, punctuation, syntax, details of style, etc. Next, the copyeditor does the substantive or copy editing, which tackles checking of factual information, content, continuity, reorganization, etc. After each, the writer will receive the edited manuscript, make the necessary changes, and return the corrected pages to the editor. The following list will help you understand the process and comply with the instructions.

Marginal Marks of Instruction		Explanation	Indicated in copy
	ℊ	Delete, take out	She wrote the boo*k. or boo/k.
	stet	Let it stand	~~She wrote the book.~~
	sp.	Spell out	She wrote (5) books.
	tr.	Transpose	She the wrote book.
	¶	Paragraph	new. ^She wrote the book.
	no ¶	No paragraph—run in	new. She wrote the book.
	(wrote /?)	Query to the author	She ^ the book.
Marginal Marks of Punctuation	⊙	Period	She wrote the book^
	^,	Comma	She wrote the book^
	;/	Semicolon	She wrote the book^
	:/	Colon	She wrote the book^so
	=/	Hyphen	She is copy^editing.
	∨'∨	Apostrophe	It is the editors^ copy.
	∨"∨ ∨"∨	Open and close quotes	She said: ^Send the proofs.^
	!/	Exclamation	Write the book^
	?/	Question mark	Did she write the book^
	1/n or 1/en	One-en dash	Pages, 24, 45, 137^8
	1/m or 1/em	One-em dash	She left 1/m she came back.
	(|)	Open and close parens	She^with help^wrote the book.
	[|]	Open and close brackets	She write^*sic*^the book.
	^2	Inferior figure (subscript)	H_2O
	∨2∨	Superior figure (superscript)	$a + b^2$

• • •

Proofreaders' Marks — *Continued*

	Mark	Meaning	Example
Marginal Marks for Spacing	⁀‿	Close up	She wr ote the book.
		Delete and close up	She wr/ote the book.
	#	Insert space	She wrote thebook.
	eq. #	Equalize the spacing	She ✓wrote ✓the✓book.
	□	Indent one em	□ She wrote the book.
	□□	Indent two ems	□□ She wrote the book.
	□□□	Indent three ems	□□□ She wrote the book.
	[	Move left as indicated	[She wrote the book.
	]	Move right as indicated	She wrote the book.]
	⌐¬	Raise as indicated	She wrote the book.
	└┘	Lower as indicated	She wrote the book.
	ld.	Insert lead between lines	Leading = space between lines.
	fl.	Flush left	[She wrote the book.
	fr.	Flush right	She wrote the book.]
	ctr.	Center	] TITLE [
Marginal Marks for Type Style	*ital.*	Set in italic	She wrote the book.
	s.c.	Set in small capitals	She wrote the book.
	caps.	Set in CAPITALS	she wrote the book.
	c. & s.c.	Set in Capitals & Small Capitals	she wrote the book.
	b.f. *or bf.*	Set in bold face	She wrote the book.
	rom.	Change from italic to roman	She wrote the *book*.
	l.c.	Set in lower case	She Wrote the Book.
	u. & l.c. or c. & l.c.	Set in Upper & Lower Case	she wrote the book.
Marginal Marks for Type Defects	⊗	Broken letters	She wrote the book.
	wf.	Wrong font	She wrote the book.
	‖	Straighten marked lines	She wrote the book. She wrote the book.
	=	Out of alignment—straighten	She wr$_o$te the book.
	↓	Push down space	She wrote the book.
	9	Turn inverted letters	˙ʞooq ǝɥʇ ǝʇoɹʍ ǝɥS

The final step will be the writer's proofreading of the typeset book pages. These are called by various names, blue lines, blues, proofs, proof pages, galleys, galley proofs. Whatever your editor calls them, proof them carefully! Find and mark all typesetting mistakes, spelling errors, words left out, sentences/paragraphs missing—or duplicated. Read carefully, mark, as necessary, with the proofreaders' symbols listed here. • • •

EVERY PAGE PERFECT

• • •

True reason in writing comes from art, not chance,
As those move easiest who have learned to dance.
'Tis not enough no harshness gives offense;
The sound must seem an echo to the sense.

—Alexander Pope, 1688-1744
From: *An Essay on Criticism*

Short Nonfiction

Manuscript Form: A To-the-Point Explanation

• • •

Magazines, newspapers, and newsletters buy articles. They want a sensational hook, a fresh slant on a solid theme, concise writing, and a dynamite conclusion that proves your premise.

What's the point?

Get to the point.

Length? Read and study the publication. Send for guidelines.

Subject? Read and study the publication. Send for guidelines.

Style? Read and study the publication. Send for guidelines.

Format? Read on.

• • •

A reminder about rights (further discussed on pages 18 and 46). A publisher actually buys only the license to publish, not the right to own the existent work. Several articles can be registered, at one time, with the Copyright Office on Form GR/PC. Recorded message/order line: 202-707-9100. There are many different rights the writer may offer to a publisher. Among them—

First Serial Rights. The one-time, first-time right to publish a work in any *one* of the publisher's periodicals (serials). First Serial Rights can be limited or expanded to specific areas and languages. See below.

First Worldwide Serial Rights. First-time, one-time right to publish a piece in *each* of the publisher's domestic and/or foreign editions, in English and/or foreign languages.

First North American Serial Rights. The first-time, one-time right to publish a work in a periodical which is distributed in both the United States of America and Canada. Can be limited to English.

One-Time Rights. Similar to First Serial Rights above, but One-Time Rights does not guarantee the publisher that he or she will be the first to publish the work. Also called Simultaneous Rights.

All Rights. The writer may not use or sell the work anywhere else, in any other country, at any time, for the life of the copyright. Sometimes this type of sale is unavoidable, but avoid it if you can.

Simultaneous Rights. This is offered when selling work to several publications with circulations that *do not overlap*. In this case, a cover letter explaining what you're doing, and why, will be necessary. Make it brief, to the point, and accurate. Also called One-Time Rights.

Second Serial Rights. Reprint rights allow a publication to print a work after it has appeared elsewhere. This right is non-exclusive and can be licensed to more than one market.

NOTE: Copyright notices, on manuscripts, may be dated or not, your choice. Dates provide proof, as to time of creation, if disputes arise. Dates may be changed, year to year, if copyright is not registered and when the piece is either unpublished or revised, updated, re-slanted, or rewritten.

SEE: An additional list of Authors' Rights on page 46.

There are two main schools of thought on query letter writing. Both have to do with the first paragraph and both have advantages.

In form number one, the writer mentions his or her article-writing credits in the first sentence. The proposed article subject, title of the article, and the name of the publication all appear in the second sentence.

In form number two, the writer begins the letter with either the actual hook contained in the article being proposed, or uses a similar attention-grabbing sentence to get the editor immediately interested in the idea.

An alternative type of greeting paragraph is also useful, but requires that you've actually met the editor face-to-face or by phone. In this letter you'd begin by saying something like: *It was so nice to meet you at . . .* ; or *Thank you very much for your help with . . .* ; or *Thank you for talking to me on the phone about . . .* This first paragraph has the advantage of acting as an introductory ice-breaker and a reminder of previous contact.

The advantage of the credits-on-line-one approach is obvious. If you are a writer with major magazine credits and tear-sheets to prove them, editors are impelled to read on.

On the other hand, if you have expertise, experience, or education in your subject (but not article writing), the subject, itself, may carry more weight in the read-on category. The exception to this is when you are not only an expert, but also a famous expert, or when you have endorsements from a famous expert.

Certain vital statistics belong in the query letter, no matter what the form. Include:

1) Name of the publication for which you're writing;
2) Name of the column or department targeted (if applicable);
3) Title of the article;
4) Length of the article (number of words);
5) Subject;
6) Focus/slant/angle/approach;
7) Research done;
8) Photos or illustrations included;
9) Endorsements by experts (if any); and
10) Reader appeal.

Query letters for short nonfiction are single spaced and have the same 1 1/4-inch margins as a manuscript. One page is preferred. Two pages are acceptable—and maximum. Author's personal letterhead, while not necessary, lends to an attractive presentation.

Address your query letter to a specific editor by name and title (if applicable). Include a self-addressed, stamped envelope (SASE) for the editor's reply or return of your letter. (Editors often reply right on your letter.) Find lists of addresses and editors' names in many publications and on the Internet. Samples of two types of query letters follow.

Larry Longhand
123 Page Boulevard, Hook, New Mexico 00000
(555) 555-5555

27 November 2004

Sidny Sylance, Features Editor
All Rights Magazine
P.O. Box AAA
Prinet, Pennsylvania 00000

Dear Mr. Sylance:

I am a writer with credits in Reader's Digest, Life, People Magazine, and others. I'd like to propose an article on the subject of sensuality at seventy titled LOVE LIVES ON, for All Rights Magazine.

It has recently occurred to me that I am seventy years old, and nothing has changed in the way I view my feelings for Martha. Pen in hand, and with full cooperation and permission, I interviewed contemporaries about the subject of sensuality and found that 90 percent of my peers had not given up on love. Interviews also include expert opinions from doctors of medicine, psychologists, and counselors.

Revelations point to the fact that over-the-hill does not necessarily mean out-of-order, which will be the focus of the story. The theme is "relax and enjoy, without worrying." Anecdotes included are sensitive and humorous.

Since your magazine is published for readers fifty and over, and since fully 100 percent of those interviewed had concerns and doubts about their own approach to sensuality, I view the article as both timely and needed.

I am prepared to write a feature article, of about 2,500 words, focusing on dispelling tension in close relationships. If you would be interested, I'd be glad to write the piece on speculation and follow any editorial suggestions you'd care to make.

Sincerely,

Larry Longhand
(555) 555-5555 - LaLo@xxx.com

Larry Younger Longhand, Jr.
321 Page Boulevard
Hook, New Mexico 00000

14 August 2003

Sydney Sylance, Jr., Editor
New Rights Magazine
P.O. Box AAA
New York, NY 00000

Dear Mr. Sylance:

"My feets too big! I wanna die!"

Scary words for a young father to hear from a five-year-old, after his son's first day at kindergarten. But given the fact that young children are cruel (without meaning to be, most of the time), and given the fact that young children are sensitive, I felt I had to find out what a parent could do to alleviate the hurt after such an episode of taunting, while disarming the threat of permanent damage to fragile psyches.

Ingenious techniques for restoring dignity and self-worth came from extensive interviews with all manner of experts in the fields of psychiatry, psychology, theology, and parenting. Word-for-word, action-by-action approaches to pinpointing the problem, defusing the anger, soothing the hurt, and guiding young children toward new and worthwhile goals in the aftermath of such incidents will be the focus of my 3,000-word article for New Rights Magazine. Photos of my son, John, will be included.

"My feets are big! That means I'll grow tall!"

Comforting words for a young father to hear from his five-year-old. The techniques revealed in CRUEL AND THE USUAL PUNISHMENT really do work--and I have a happy six-year-old to prove it. I would be glad to write this article for your consideration and follow any guidelines you suggest.

Sincerely,

Larry Younger Longhand
(555) 555-5555 - LaLo@xxx.com

Section Two: Article Submission

• • •

No matter what type article you're writing, from the ever-popular "List," to the personal-opinion essay, to the always-interesting "General Interest," the manuscript format for every submission stays the same.

Unlike book-length nonfiction, short nonfiction does not require a cover sheet. Similar information is placed on the first page of the article itself. See page 8.

Several subjects that always sell very well are about better ways to:

1) Cope;
2) Overcome problems;
3) Enjoy more rewarding relationships;
4) Travel;
5) Live;
6) Succeed;
7) Make money;
8) Invest;
9) Save;
10) Eat;
11) Diet;
12) Get beautiful;
13) Stay healthy; and . . .
14) Be a better parent.

True crime, biographies, and popular psychology are also hot sellers. But even these nationally appealing blockbusters won't sell if your approach isn't new and fresh. In the slant department, think of controversy first. The pros and cons of timely causes, political disagreements, questionably successful or new medical treatments, wars, and other arguments will most always get a thorough reading.

Whenever possible and/or appropriate, interview experts in the field of your subject. These sources of quotes and information lend credibility to your writing and can sometimes lead you, unexpectedly and happily, into the disputatious arena where experts disagree.

Always research a subject in depth. Extensive study can lead you to new article ideas and new markets. Keep all research materials and leads well organized by subject for easy reference and quick access.

Remember, articles require careful checking of factual information and extensive investigative research. Fiction has no place in short nonfiction. Although the piece may contain some conjecture on the part of the writer and other sources, it must also reflect all sides of an issue. Readers might disagree with you, your research, and your experts, but you should give them something new to think about in everything you write.

A cover letter always accompanies an article submission. Make it very short and to the point. A sample follows.

Barnhart Fieldman
Starr Route 7
Sink City, FL 00000

12 July 2002

Talbat Trapper, New Products Editor
Roaring Mouse Monthly
1500 Runnaway Avenue
Columbus, GA 00000

Dear Mr. Trapper:

Enclosed is the first story in the series of articles we discussed for your column, MOUSETRAPS: FRIEND OR FOE? At the time we last spoke, Dr. Eldon Richards, of International Center for Rodent Studies, had agreed to be interviewed regarding the newest in mousetrap technologies. Unfortunately, Dr. Richards was called away suddenly--a crisis in a cheese factory, I understand--and was unavailable for the interview. In his place, I contacted Dr. Juanita Arroyo, an expert in the field of rodent behavior, and she was kind enough to give me the information I required. This unexpected change of sources doesn't alter the basic fabric of this first article, however, nor does it alter the schedule for the articles that follow.

I've enjoyed the opportunity to write for Roaring Mouse Monthly, and I hope you'll keep me in mind for future assignments. As always, I will be happy to make any editorial changes you may wish to suggest.

Sincerely,

Barnhart Fieldman
555-555-5555 - BaFi@xxx.com

E-mail Submissions— Many editors now accept pasted and attached e-mail queries, articles, and photos. When pasting copy into an e-mail, there are a few things to remember to avoid 'garbage' transmission. 1) Use straight "dumb" quote marks, not curly “smart” quotes. 2) Do not underline. 3) Do not use *italics*. 4) Use a blank line between paragraphs instead of a tabbed indent. 5) Avoid ALL Option, Control, or Alt + Key characters, like ©. When sending attachments, make sure your copy is saved in the word processing program required by the editor and use standard EPP format. Photos should be sent in the format required, usually JPEG or TIFF.

Barnhart Fieldman
Starr Route 7
Sink City, FL 00000
(555) 555-5555 - BaFi@xxx.com
SS# 555-55-5555

Article for Roaring Mouse Monthly
Three Pages
About 600 words
First North American Serial Rights
© Fieldman, 2002

THEREBY HANGS A TAIL:

MOUSETRAPS THAT SAVE LIVES

by

Barnhart Fieldman

PART ONE: HEAD AND WHISKERS ABOVE THE REST

Margins for short nonfiction are 1 1/4 inches or larger, top, bottom, right, and left. Single space the two blocks of information in the upper left and right corners. Type the TITLE in capital letters, and center it. The word "by" is one double space below the TITLE and in lower case. Center the Author's Name one double space below the word "by," and type in upper and lower case letters. If you're using a pen name, drop another double space below your legal name and center w/a (means writing as) followed by your Pen Name. Ten to twelve lines of text on the first page gives plenty of white space above the title for the editor's notes, so space your headings accordingly. Right edges of the text are ragged, never justified.

The text of the article begins two double spaces below the Author's

Name or last heading line. Double space all the text throughout the article.

Use only white, twenty-pound bond typing paper or good quality photocopy or laser printer paper. Tractor-feed printer paper must be of the clean-edge or clean-tear variety, unless the submission will be photocopied. Always tear these fan-fold sheets apart before mailing. Always keep a copy of your original manuscript. Mail either a good photocopy, laser printout, or ink-jet printout. Electronic and soft copy submissions (on computer floppy disk) are now accepted by many publishers. Query about system requirements for modem or disk submissions.

When using a typewriter, remember: Without exception, editors prefer pica type to elite type. Always use a clear, plain text, pica typeface that gives 10 characters to the inch. Writers working on a computer should always choose a serif font that is similar in appearance and size to the font used in this book. Herein, the font is 12-point (size), New Century Schoolbook, used on a Macintosh PowerPC. (My copy is printed on a Hewlett Packard LaserJet 4 ML printer.) Never use italic, calligraphic, script, or any other fancy type.

Place the running header at the top of the second page and every subsequent page, 1/2 inch below the top edge of the paper. Right and left margins for the header are the same as for the text. A KEY WORD from the TITLE appears on the left, typed in capital letters. The author's legal last name, one dash (-), and the page number go on the right.

Again, margins for the text are 1 1/4 inches all the way around. There will be twenty-five lines of text on each full page, making the total word count approximately two hundred fifty words per page. Margins at the bottom of pages may vary somewhat, depending on your choice of type. Don't worry about this, as long as the space is 1 1/4 inches or more.

Begin your article with a hook. A hook grabs the reader's interest and makes him or her want to continue reading. A hook also sets the tone of your article: Humorous, scholarly, folksy, or condemning, etc. Here are a few examples of opening hooks.

• • •

Through the latest advance in solar technology, you can throw away your old mousetraps, and without fuss or bloodshed, never again see another rascally rodent!

• • •

My daughter wanted to name them. My son wanted to feed them imported Brie. My husband wanted to wait until the Pied Piper showed up before we did anything. I wanted every mouse out of my house by sundown. And one way or another, sooner or later, I always get what I want.

• • •

Poor Richard. The world not only beat a path to solar mousetrap inventor Richard Yazzie's door, it beat the laboratory door right down on top of the unsuspecting Man of Mice.

• • •

Begin with a hook, then finish the nonfiction article with the symbol ### or -30- signifying the end. Type ### or -30- centered and two double spaces below the last line of text. Pages of an article manuscript may be paper-clipped together for mailing.

###

Section Three: Fillers

• • •

Fillers are just what the name implies. They fill up space. Almost every periodical has leftover corners and crannies where short, interesting tidbits of information can be inserted. *Reader's Digest* devotes entire pages to these brief, sometimes humorous, sometimes solemn, little pieces. "Humor in Uniform" and "Life in these United States" are two of several good areas to study for style and content.

Departments for fillers are variously called columns, bulletin boards, regular features, and almanacs. Carefully study several issues of the publications for which you want to write. An entire year's worth of issues will be the best number to analyze. Avoid sending work on a subject that's been used in the past twelve months.

Send for guidelines to find out what type of work is being bought, how the publisher wants it written, style and length requirements, and deadline information. Length for fillers can be anywhere from 40 or 50 words to 500 words. Some magazines buy photos and/or illustrations with their fillers. The specific publication's needs must always be your guide.

Almost any kind of information can go into a filler, from advice about an interesting hobby or craft, to simple, rhyming verse. Three sure ways to find out what a magazine wants: Read several issues of the publication, check *Writer's Market*, and send for the guidelines.

The market for fillers is an excellent place for beginning writers to start. Then, when querying an editor about an article you want to write, you can refer to a published filler as a writing credit. (You don't have to say your credits in *Redbook* and *Esquire* are for 75-word fillers; simply say that you have credits in *Redbook* and *Esquire*.)

A filler can be about almost anything, as long as it fits the style and content of the publication and the interests of its readers. For instance:

1) Anecdotes;
2) Cartoons;
3) Facts;
4) Short humor;
5) Newsbreaks;
6) Light verse;
7) Gags;
8) Tips;
9) Helpful hints;
10) Poetry;
11) Illustrations; and
12) Photos.

Format for presenting the filler is straightforward and easy. Use the standard business letter form, fax, or e-mail, whatever the guidelines call for. When sending more than one filler, type one filler per page.

Freda Fuller
Trivia Road, Route 1
Grand Bits, New Jersey 00000
555-555-5555
SS# 000-00-0000

Filler for Deadline Magazine
One Page
21 words
All Rights
Copyright by Fuller, 1999

Date

Quigley Shortzs, "Writer's Nightmare" Editor
Deadline Magazine
678 Fort Kaynox Drive
Last Chance, Massachusetts 00000

Dear Mr. Shortzs:

Please consider the following for your "Writer's Nightmare" column.

Typos are like cockroaches. No matter how many holes you plug, they're gonna sneak back in when the lights go out.

Thank you for your attention.

Sincerely,

Freda Fuller
(555) 555-5555 - FrFu@xxx.com

{Note: Mail a filler submission in this form, by first class mail, or fax, if fax submissions are accepted. Always follow publishers' guidelines.}

{Note: When submitting by e-mail, type the name of the department or column (if applicable) in the "Subject" slot. Other information, such as your name, address, phone number, etc., will be part of your message.}

{Note: If fillers are over 200 words, use the short nonfiction article format shown on pages 8-10.}

Section Four: News Release

• • •

Writing publicity for your organization or club can be a rewarding experience, especially if your local newspaper is the friendly type that tries to be helpful in the community-service arena. Friendly or not, the newspaper probably has some guidelines you'll need to follow in order to get your news release into print. Follow the publication's guidelines exactly.

No guidelines available? Below are some tips that will help you, in case your paper doesn't furnish the specifics. Two release samples follow.

Always start the piece by naming the upcoming event, telling what it is, when it's scheduled to take place, and where it will be held. Put the most important information as near to the beginning as possible. If material must be cut from the copy to make it fit the space available, it will be cut from the bottom. The least important information should always be in the last paragraphs and sentences. Logical progression is the key here.

News releases are printed free of charge. As a general rule, you can leave your carnival-barker hat on the hook by the door. You are writing news, not an ad. Newspapers *sell* their advertising space, they don't give it away. They are perfectly justified in refusing to print a news release that's really just a poorly disguised advertisement. The same refusal to print is true of a release that needs considerable editing or rewrite. Newspapers also have strict deadlines. Find out what they are. Meet them!

When reporting a club meeting or the like, be sure to attribute any quotes to the proper person to avoid implications of editorial opinion. Limit lists of names, such as new officers, etc., to only the most important. You may suggest a headline for your copy, but don't expect them to use it. This task is traditionally reserved for editors.

You may find the need to prepare news releases for your personal activities as a writer. Authors, with books coming out, will want to send news releases to newspapers, libraries, radio and television stations for scheduled signings or other public appearances. Any public event is worth the time it takes to write and mail interesting and informative news releases. People who didn't even think they would, will want to know about and attend your talks or readings at libraries, local businesses, churches, and community events. Would-be writers will want to know about classes, seminars, and workshops you'll be teaching. Always include information about your connection to the area visited, when appropriate.

Authors' press kits are often sent along with a release. If press kits and releases are not furnished by your current publisher's publicity department, it's easy to make up your own. Use attractive pocket folders that hold 8 1/2-by-11 sheets. Inside include a professionally done, black and white photograph (any standard size), a business card, a book cover, one page of biographical information that pertains to the book's subject or setting, and your news release. (Always ask your editor for book cover overruns.) Add other info as desired; copies of reviews, endorsements, testimonials. Send press kits in manila envelopes with a cover letter.

NEWS RELEASE: For Immediate Release

Contact: Sammy Slicer
Phone: 555-5555 daytime
E-mail: SaSl@xxx.com

Quarterly meeting of the Sandbaggers Anonymous Pack

Sandbaggers Anonymous Pack will meet for a Bingo, Bango, Bongo tournament and burger cookout on April 6th, 8 a.m., at the Deadly Rough and Gulch Golf Course, 321 Liars' Lane South. For more information or a reservation, contact Sammy at 555-5555 or e-mail SaSl@xxx.com.

Bring your own clubs and condiments. Golf carts will be provided, by the SAPs, to speed play. "Two sets of Bocce balls will also be available for an afternoon of unforgettable family entertainment," says President Slicer.

A business meeting is set for later in the evening, if anyone cares to discuss business at that time.

-30-

E-mail Submissions— Some newspapers now accept pasted and attached e-mail queries, articles, photos, and news releases. To repeat the info on page 7— When pasting copy into an e-mail, there are a few things to remember to avoid 'garbage' transmission. 1) Use straight "dumb" quote marks, not curly "smart" quotes. 2) Do not underline. 3) Do not use *italics*. 4) Use a blank line between paragraphs instead of a tabbed indent. 5) Avoid ALL Option, Control, or Alt + Key characters, like ©. When sending attachments, make sure your copy is saved in the word processing program required by the editor and use standard *Every Page Perfect* format. Photos should be sent in the format required, usually JPEG or TIFF.

FOR IMMEDIATE RELEASE

News Release Contact: Sue Smith; 555-555-5555 - SuSm@xxx.com

Award-winning, Best-selling Author Reveals Secrets of Success

Novelist Mary Elizabeth Lynn will unveil the techniques for selling your work to top-paying markets during her highly-regarded, Write To $ell Fiction Workshop at the Greyfeathers Lodge at Sapillo Crossing near Silver City, New Mexico, October 26 to 28, 2001. "If you've dreamed of being published," Lynn says, "or if you've ever said, 'I ought to write a book about that,' then this workshop is for you." This yearly, Halloween-weekend presentation in the Silver City area, using Lynn's proven step-by-step approach, will teach how to craft the perfect story, from short to book-length fiction, query editors, understand contracts, get an agent, and everything else you must know to $ell your fiction!

Mary Elizabeth Lynn is author of twelve novels and the nonfiction text, Every Page Perfect, A Full-Size Writer's Manual for Manuscript Format and Submission Protocol, Fourth Edition (order at <www.writers center.com>). Her latest project, The Writer's Business Bible, co-authored with her husband Ted, is now in the hands of their agent.

Lynn has won the prestigious Parris Award for her writing, teaching skills, and her efforts in co-founding the Albuquerque-based, 1,200+ member SouthWest Writers. To receive workshop information call: 505-388-3813 or e-mail mary@writerscenter.com.

# # #

Section Five: Checklists

• • •

Query Letters •

1. #10 business envelope
   Addressed to specific editor
   Return address
   Sufficient postage
2. #10 business envelope (for reply)
   Addressed to the writer
   Stamped
   Folded in thirds to insert
3. Stamped postcard (optional with queries). Example, page 44.
   Addressed to writer (for verification of query arrival)
4 Query letter

Articles •

1. 9x12 manila envelope
   Addressed to specific editor
   Return address
   Sufficient postage
2. 9x12 manila envelope (for return of manuscript)
   Sufficient postage (paper clipped to the cover letter)
   Folded in half to insert
3. Stamped postcard. Example, page 44.
   Addressed to writer (for verification of article arrival)
4. Cover letter (with return postage paper clipped to it)
5. Article manuscript

Fillers •

1. #10 business envelope
   Addressed to specific editor or department
   Return address
   Sufficient postage
2. Filler(s)
   One per page

News Releases •

1. Hand carry, mail in #10 envelope, fax or e-mail (if allowed)
   Addressed to specific editor or department
   Return address
   Sufficient postage
2. News release

Short Fiction

Manuscript Form: A Short Explanation

• • •

Since short fiction is rarely queried, it is extremely important that the copy looks perfectly professional and the cover letter is polite, brief, and to the point. Type all manuscripts on one side of white, twenty-pound bond or equivalent quality paper. Information necessary for the processing of the manuscript must appear on the first page of the short story.

Let's start from the outside and move in. Address the envelope to a specific editor, by name if possible, and the correct publisher or publication. If the editor's name is impossible to obtain, address to the publisher or publication, attention to the Fiction or Story Editor. Be sure your full name and complete return address appear on the mailing envelope. For return of your manuscript, enclose either a self-addressed envelope (SAE) with sufficient postage paper-clipped in place, or a self-addressed, stamped envelope (SASE) with postage attached in the usual manner.

Though some guidelines say a cover letter isn't necessary, it's always right when: The story is unsolicited; when you've talked to an editor and want to remind her/him of the conversation; when you know the editor personally; when selling simultaneous rights; or when the subject is so timely or pertinent to the audience you feel bound to let the editor know that it's in the publication's best interest to consider the story immediately.

Another reminder about rights. A publisher actually buys only the right to publish (usually in English), not to *own* the actual work. There are several different rights the author may offer to a publisher. Among them—

First Serial Rights. The one-time, first-time right to publish a work in any *one* of the publisher's periodicals (serials). First Serial Rights can be limited or expanded to specific areas and languages. See below.

First Worldwide Serial Rights. First-time, one-time right to publish a piece in *each* of the publisher's domestic and/or foreign editions, in English and/or specific foreign languages.

First North American Serial Rights. The first-time, one-time right to publish a work in a periodical which is distributed in both the United States of America and Canada. Can be limited to English.

One-Time Rights. Similar to First Serial Rights above, but One-Time Rights does not guarantee the publisher that he or she will be the first to publish the work. Also called Simultaneous Rights.

All Rights. The writer may not use or sell the work anywhere else, in any other country, at any time, for the life of the work. Sometimes this type of sale is unavoidable, but avoid it if you can.

Simultaneous Rights. This is offered when selling work to several publications with circulations that *do not overlap*. In this case, a cover letter explaining what you're doing and why will be necessary. Make it brief, to the point, and accurate. Also called One-Time Rights.

Section One: Short Story Submission • Read the target publication. Send for story guidelines. Write it. Mail it. A format example follows.

Wanda Wright
P.O. Drawer AAA
Storey, South Carolina 00000

February 1, 2002

Edith Reedith, Fiction Editor
Real Resistance Magazine
P.O. Box XXX
Lybary, Louisiana 00000

Dear Ms. Reedith,

Thank you very much for sending the guidelines for the Real Resistance Magazine's "Mini-Mystery," "Angel Romance," and "Supernatural Suspense" short fiction.

I wrote the story, THE MYTH OF THYME, because of an article, in a recent edition of The Wall Street Journal, about a brand new research that proves certain herbs have miraculous healing powers. Thyme is among them! I hope you think THE MYTH is both timely and appropriate for "Angel Romance."

THE MYTH OF THYME deals with a miraculous healing and accurately reflects up-to-the-minute scientific research, while heroine and hero fall in love. I'll make any changes you think necessary.

Thank you again.

Yours,

Wanda Wright
(555) 555-5555 - WaWr@xxx.com

Wanda Wright
P.O. Drawer AAA
Storey, South Carolina 00000
(555) 555-5555 - WaWr@xxx.com
SS# 000-00-0000

Short Story for Real Resistance Magazine
Nine Pages
About 2,000 words
First North American Serial Rights
© by Wanda Wright, 1999

THE MYTH OF THYME

by

Wanda Wright

The information, in the upper left corner on the first page, looks remarkably like that found on most fiction manuscripts. It tells the editor that you know who you are, where you live, how you can be reached, and that you want to be paid. (The social security number is the universally understood code for: "Send check by return mail.")

The difference on the first page of short fiction begins in the upper right corner. Here you must tell the editor that you know what you're doing. Yes, Real buys short fiction. Yes, 2,000 words will fit nicely on nine pages with generous margins, and Real buys 2,000-word short stories. Yes, of course, I want to keep all the rights to my story except your license to print one time. Yes, the story is my idea (©) and I can prove it in a court of law. The word Copyright can be used instead of the © symbol.

Ten to twelve lines of text make a nice-looking Page One. Another happy event, as promised on the first page: THE END appears after the thirteenth line of text, on this last page, numbered nine. Eight full pages. Twenty-five lines per page. About 250 words per page, using pica type or a 12- to 14-point, serif-style, computer font. Voilà! 2,000 words.

The first page is not numbered. On every subsequent page, the page number appears in the right corner, after your last name and a hyphen (-). The KEY WORD from the title, in the left corner, unmistakably identifies each page as belonging to the same work. Right and left margins for the running header are 1 1/4 inches. Top running header margin is 1/2 inch.

Text on all pages, following page one, begins 1 1/4 inches from the top edge of the paper. Right, left, and bottom text margins are also 1 1/4 inches or larger. Left margin for the text is justified. Right margin is ragged.

Yes, the record is broken and keeps repeating: Generous Margins!

THE END

REMEMBER: You can go to all lengths! These are the standards, but publications vary. *Always send for guidelines!*

Short Short-Adult: 1,500 words or fewer (5-6 manuscript pages)
Short Story-Adult: 1,500 to 10,000 words (5-40 manuscript pages)
Short Story-Children to Young Adult: 200 to 2,000 words (1-8 MS pages)
Novella / Novelette: 30,000 to 50,000 words (100-200 manuscript pages)

NOTE: Send loose manuscript pages only. Never bind a short story submission in any way—no paperclips, staples, folders, binders, or any other page-constraining devices—unless requested in the guidelines.

HOT TIP: Read *Fiction Writer's Market* to learn submission policies of publishers that buy short fiction. Some require presubmission queries. Double-check editors' names in the mastheads of your target periodicals. Read *many* stories in your chosen publication(s) to make sure your story fits all requirements. Send for guidelines!

Section Two: Checklists

• • •

Short Fiction •

1. Mailing envelope, 9x12 manila
   Send short fiction flat unless it's three pages or under. Three pages or fewer may be folded in thirds, like a business letter, and sent in a #10 business-size envelope. "Flat" is preferred.
2. Mailing label for 9x12 envelope
   Type or write both recipient's and sender's address and Attach appropriately.
3. Postage
   Make sure it's sufficient, if you're mailing from home.
4. Return envelope, 9x12 manila, or SASE #10 (folded for insertion)
5. Mailing label (if using a 9x12 manila envelope)
   Fill out label completely and attach to the envelope.
6. Return postage
   Either paper clipped to the envelope or attached in the usual manner.
7. Verification postcard, with postage. Example, page 44.
   Addressed to you (for validation of story arrival)
8. Cover letter (if included)
9. Manuscript

E-mail Submissions— Some short fiction editors now accept pasted and attached e-mail queries and short stories. If publication guidelines solicit e-mail copy, follow all instructions concerning pasted text or attachments.

When pasting copy into an e-mail, there are a few things to remember to avoid 'garbage' transmission.

1) Use straight "dumb" quote marks, not curly “smart” quotes.
2) Do not <u>underline</u>.
3) Do not use *italics*.
4) Use a blank line between paragraphs instead of a tabbed indent.
5) Avoid ALL Option, Control, or Alt + Key characters, like ©.

When sending attachments, make sure your copy is saved in the word processing program required by the editor/publication, and use standard *Every Page Perfect* format.

Poetry & Verse

Manuscript Form: Poetry and Verse

• • •

THE NORM

Privileged lines,
Poetry shines,
Centered on bond,
Your couplets respond.

Poetry, verse,
Greetings disperse.
Some should arrive
On cards 3 by 5.

Models must work,
Thank-yous must perk,
Mechanicals twist . . .
Then check the checklist.

• • •

Section One: Poetry Submission • Just as typesetters worry about such things as indenting rhyming lines, to keep rhyme scheme clear, and numbering every fifth and tenth lines in verse plays, poets should be concerned about how best to display the poetry they're writing. When putting poetry into a book or magazine, the typesetter is as faithful as possible to the poet's intention, so take care with your presentation.

Construct the poem in exactly the way you want to see it on the page of a book or magazine, especially if the shape of it helps the reader to understand the rhythm or visualize the idea.

Study the market to which you intend to sell. If a magazine publishes only short, rhyming poems, don't send long, non-rhyming free verse. The converse is also true.

Write one poem per page, unless the poem is longer than one page, of course. Several poems can usually be sent at once, but a request for guidelines is always a good idea if you're not sure of editorial requirements.

Single space the lines, double space between stanzas. Short poems can be double spaced, with two double-spaced lines between stanzas. Some editors like this, some insist on it. Place your name, address, phone number, e-mail, SS#, and © notice in the upper right corner of each manuscript 1 1/4 inches from the top and right edges of the paper. Always title your poem. For long poems, use a running header on the subsequent pages and note the line count below the copyright notice.

A cover letter is rarely used, but, if you have powerful credits, feel free to note them in a *very* brief letter. Consult guidelines if in doubt.

Name
Address
City, State Zip Code
Social Security Number

Date

Editor's Name and Title
Publication
Address
City, State Zip Code

Dear Editor's Name:

I am a poet with credits in Guideposts Magazine, Reader's Digest, and Good Housekeeping. Please consider the following poems, PRETTY POEM and ODE TO A POEM TOO LONG TO FIT ON A SINGLE PAGE, for your "Poet's Corner" column.

Thank you for your attention.

Sincerely,

Peot's's Name
Daytime Phone Number - E-mail Address

Poet's Full Legal Name
Address
City, State Zip Code
Daytime Phone Number
E-mail Address
Social Security Number
© by Poet's Name, Year

PRETTY POEM

by

Poet's Name

Remember,
Poems can be
Visual as well as
Poetic. Always make
Poems look neat on the page.

Each stanza is set apart by a double line.
The first words of every line are very often
Capitalized. And, no matter how short, never
Put two poems on the same page. If your poem
Is longer than one page, always break between two

Stanzas, no matter what!!! Never leave the first line of
A stanza alone at the bottom of a page. It might get lonely
There, and will definitely throw the editor off the rhythm you
Intended. A rhyming dictionary and handbooks for poets and/or song-
Writers can help you with the many details that I haven't room for here.

Reda Rime
w/a Wendel Werse
47 Browning Place
Barrett, MI 00000
(555) 555-5555
WeWe@xxx.com
SS# 000-00-0000

51 Lines

ODE TO A POEM TOO
LONG TO FIT ON A SINGLE
PAGE

by

Reda Rime

w/a Wendel Werse

Poems that will spread
To more than one page
Take the same headings
On the page as short poems,
Except for the <u>line count</u>
Beneath your personal
Information.

Double space between
Stanzas.
Punctuate as you wish.

In modern poetry,
Stanzas may be any
Length.
They may even vary
within the same poem.

That's okay.
Whose poem is it,
Anyway?

Play any way
You want with the
Margins.

Ragged,
        Rigid, or
                Rolling.

Page breaks should
Come between stanzas,
Even if that leaves a
Large lower margin.

But never cheat!
The top and bottom margins
Of your poem should always be
At least 1 1/4 inches.

Just be sure to put a
KEY WORD from the
Title in the running
Header, about 1/2 inch
From the top of the
Page.

The KEY WORD belongs
About 1 1/4 inches from
The left edge of the
Paper, regardless of
The margins of the
Poem.

Your last name, a
Dash, and the page
Number go on the same
Line, ending at about
1 1/4 inches from the
Right edge of the
Paper.

• • •

Haunting helps—especially if it's the card racks you're haunting. Studying the latest trends in card lines, noticing what intrigues others who are browsing beside you, and asking clerks what people are buying helps focus your ideas toward a selling market.

Send no fewer than five ideas per submission, unless guidelines suggest otherwise. The standard maximum is fifteen. Most greeting card publishers have guidelines and/or market lists they'll send out for an SASE (self-addressed, stamped envelope). Some publishers require a signed release form (guaranteeing original, unpublished work). Ask for a copy when you send for the guidelines.

Unless you're proposing (and they're buying) an entire series, many companies buy all rights to your material. A series would incorporate a character and/or theme and include other products in the line. This gives the author some negotiating power in the rights department.

Type your verses on either 3x5- or 4x6-inch cards or pieces of white twenty-pound bond, copy, or laser paper cut to size. Always put your name, address, phone number, and e-mail on the back of every card. For your own records, it's a good idea to come up with some sort of filing system and/or code for your submissions to avoid sending the same ideas to the same publisher more than once. Keep a copy of every card you send out!

Some companies will not accept unsolicited ideas. Send a letter of application describing your credits, experience, education and/or expertise, or a résumé. If interested, the editor will ask to see examples of your work.

Besides the big-two companies, American Greetings and Hallmark, there are many smaller greeting card companies from which to choose your target market. According to an Amberly Greeting Cards executive, the words are the most important part of the card. Don't worry if you're not an artist. Don't worry if you can't illustrate your own ideas. Universal sentiment is the all-important ingredient. And a few tips—

• • •

Never send simultaneous submissions, unless you know that each publisher allows them. Send for guidelines!

Always put your best ideas on top of your submission package.

Always check and double-check your spelling and grammar.

Always spend time reading cards and learning about trends. New and clever ways to twist old thoughts can often sell as well as new ideas.

Always send seasonal material a year in advance, unless other requirements are stated in the guidelines.

Always enclose an SASE with your submission and correspondence.

Always send what the company is buying. Send for guidelines!

Never send rhymes to companies that don't publish them.

Remember, there is a tremendous need for creative and original ideas in the greeting card market. If you can say something about life in a fresh, new way, this business is for you!

Name
Address
City, State Zip Code

Date

Editor's Name, Title (if any)
Greeting Card Company
Address
City, State Zip Code

Dear Editor's Name:

Since the world has been shrinking, while I've been growing up, I've collected impressions and written sentiments appropriate for sharing, on any occasion, among all human beings, no matter what racial, ethnic, religious, or other differences have separated them in the past.

I began my educational experience in Oklahoma's heartland, where your religious affiliation is as important as your political party. Schooling continued in New Mexico, in a pageant of three peoples, Native American, Mexican, Anglo. My first college English class was taken in Tokyo, Japan, at the University of Maryland Far East Division, from a Japanese professor, of the Buddhist persuasion, whose mother was Methodist and father was Shinto, and who had studied with Bertrand Russell at Trinity College in Britain. Graduate and postgraduate studies continued in such diverse locations as Taiwan, California, Florida, Colorado, New York, and Texas, while coming full circle back to Oklahoma and New Mexico.

My writing experience is similarly eclectic, including published novels (in several genres), book-length nonfiction, articles, poetry, short stories, and fillers. A brief bio, focusing on my publishing credits is enclosed.

A portfolio of sample sentiments can be mailed immediately, upon your request, and I will be happy to sign a release form, disclosure contract, or submission agreement, to assure you that my work is original and has not been submitted elsewhere.

Thank you for your attention.

Sincerely,

Writer's Name
Daytime Phone Number - E-mail Address

Name
Address
City, State Zip Code
Social Security Number

Date

Editor's Name, Title (if any)
Greeting Card Company
Address
City, State Zip Code

Dear Editor's Name:

Please consider the enclosed seven unrhymed verses for use in your "Can't Get You Out'a My Heart" line of greeting cards. I envision "love at first sight" illustrations of man and woman running into each other in several different circumstances such as: Walking along a crowded street; diving into opposite ends of the same swimming pool and coming up face to face in the center; backing out of doorways on opposite sides of a hallway and turning to bump into each other; skydiving; skiing; water cooler meeting; surgeon and her patient; or any similar chance meetings you see as fitting and appropriate.

SASE is furnished for your convenience in returning the ideas, if they do not fit your present requirements.

Thank you for your attention.

Sincerely,

Writer's Name
Daytime Phone Number
E-mail Address

Greeting Card Submission: 3x5 Card Example •

Author's Full Legal Name
Address
City, State Zip Code
(Area Code) Phone Number
E-mail Address
Social Security Number

Your personal filing code message or number

Example shows both sides of one of the 3x5-card submissions that might accompany the cover letter on the previous page.

Exactly what do you think I've been doing all your life?

I've been thinking about you . . .

And didn't even know it--

Till today!

Always send for guidelines and/or market lists! Follow guidelines carefully. Study every card rack you see for trends, fads, techniques, and styles.

Section Three: Models

• • •

There are three types of greeting cards that need more attention than a simple index card; the mechanical, the attachment, and the studio.

The mechanical card has moving parts. Pop-ups, slide-outs, and rotating wheels are just a few of the possibilities in this category. Whatever your design, a working dummy must be submitted in order to be considered for purchase.

The attachment is a card that includes an attached object, in addition to paper and sentiment. An example might be an actual ribbon attached to the drawing of a brightly wrapped birthday present.

Studio cards are those #10 envelope-size, usually humorous greetings on heavy paper stock. Studio ideas should be sent out on dummies, sheets of paper that are folded to about the size of an actual card. If you're an artist, sketch in your visual design. If you're not an artist, feel free to suggest, but leave the drawing to the pros. Print or type your copy on the outside and/or inside of the dummy. The example on Pages 36 and 37 shows three panels.

Whatever your style, the following questions will help you get your ideas to flowing. Did you know that—

Ninety percent of all greeting cards are bought by women?

There are many markets for the fresh, new-and-truly humorous look at everyday life?

Card companies may buy text for an assortment of other products such as bumper stickers, plaques, puzzles, postcards, promotions, slogans, gift books, T-shirts, novelties, notepads, calendars, invitations, announcements, nightshirts, coffee mugs, wearable buttons, key tags, gift bags, posters, bookmarks, bookplates, quote books, aprons, pillowcases, scrolls, and more?

Some companies target a particular audience, excluding all others?

When writing, you should always keep in mind the person who'll be sending the card, the person who will receive it, and the situation or occasion that precipitates the purchase?

Some companies want no poetry?

There are publishers that work 18 months ahead of a season?

An in-store preview of cards in your target card line is the best way to learn the market and avoid rejection?

A select number of publishers are willing to work with new writers to help them develop their ideas?

Non-working samples of the mechanical, the attachment, and studio submissions follow.

Mechanical •

Outside panel

I'd even climb a mountain just to see you one more time!

Instructions to the writer: For a working mechanical, cut along the line of the spiral. Glue a paper tab to the center that says "PULL." By pulling the tab straight up, you can create the effect of a mountain. Crude, perhaps, but the visual idea of even an inelegant mechanical will come across to the editor, whether or not you can draw.

Inside panel

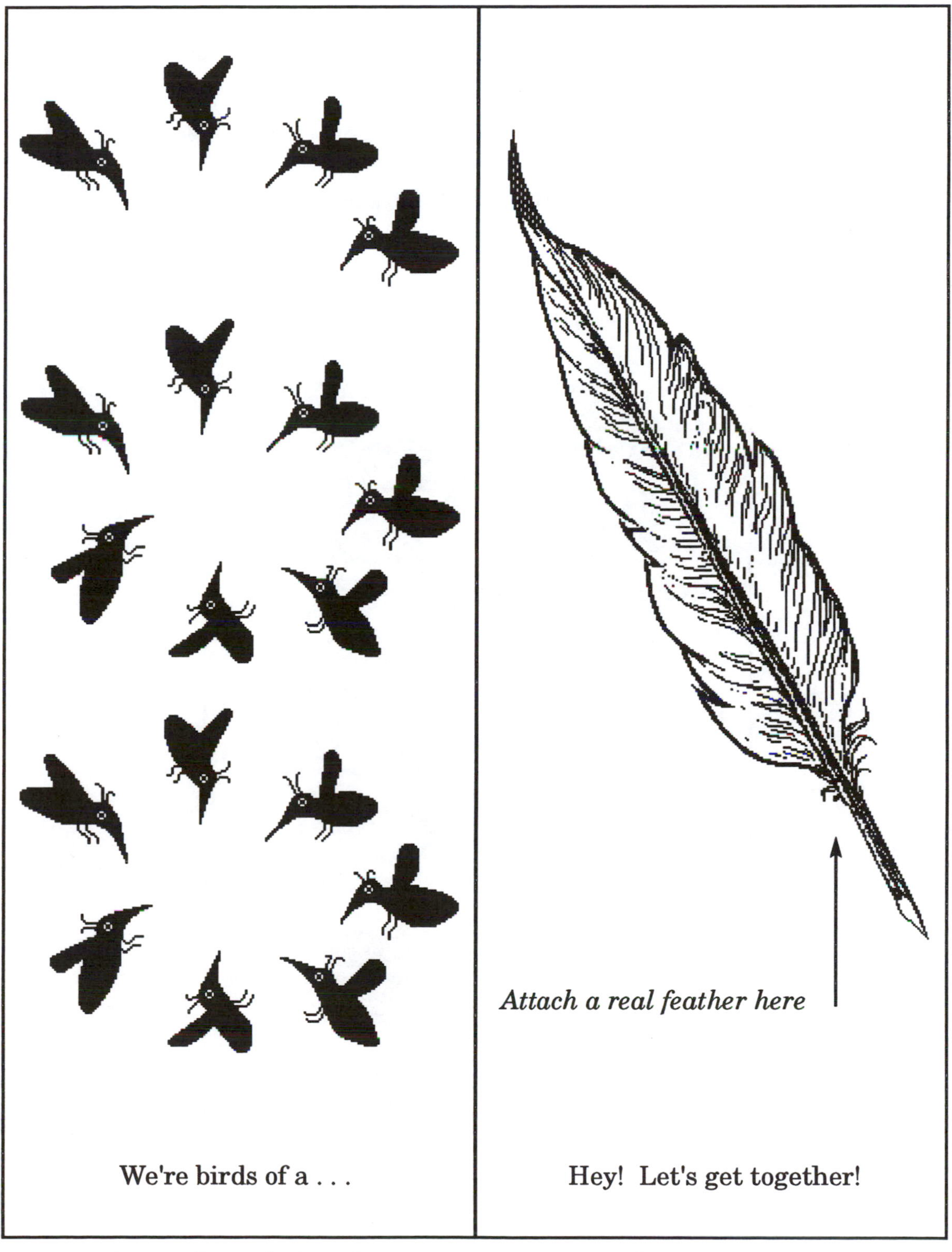

We're birds of a . . .
Attach a real feather here
Hey! Let's get together!

Front Outside Panel

Right Inside Panel

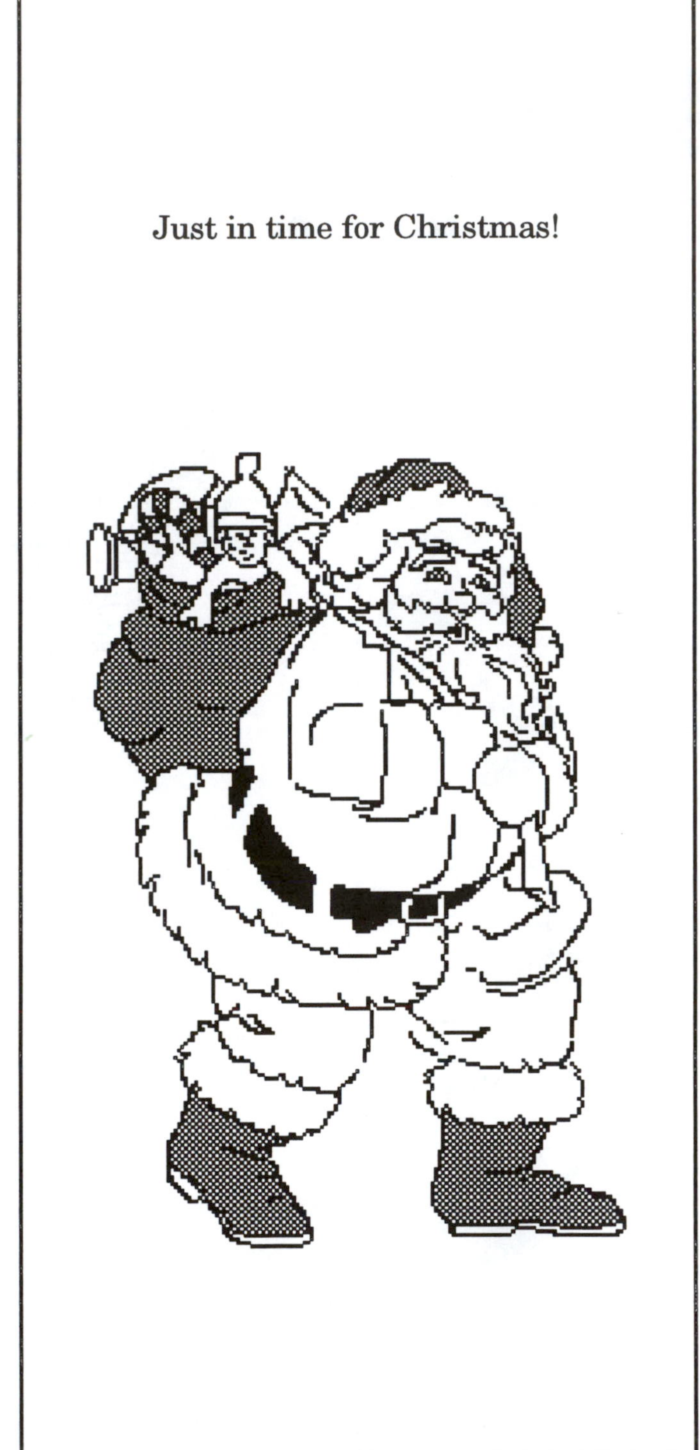
Just in time for Christmas!

Front Outside Panel

Inside Left Panel

Inside Right Panel

Early, I know.

But I took your advice . . .

And got organized!

In July!

Thanks my friend.

Section Four: Checklists

• • •

Poetry and Verse •

1. #10 business envelope (for up to five pages) or
   9x12 manila envelope
   - Addressed to specific editor (whenever possible)
   - Return address
   - Sufficient postage
2. #10 business envelope or 9x12 manila (for return or reply)
   - Addressed to you
   - Stamped
   - Folded for easy enclosure
3. Postcard w/ postage
   - Addressed to you (for verification of manuscript arrival)
4. Cover letter
5. Poetry

Greeting Cards •

1. #10 business envelope or
   9x12 manila envelope (as appropriate)
   - Addressed to specific editor
   - Return address
   - Sufficient postage
2. #10 business envelope or 9x12 manila
   - Addressed to you
   - Stamped
   - Folded for easy enclosure
3. Signed release form (if required)
4. Postcard with postage
   - Addressed to you (for verification of submission arrival)
5. Cover letter
6. 3x5 cards and/or models

NOTE: Packaging instructions can differ among various publishers. Follow the checklist above, unless individual mailing directions are supplied by the company. If your submission is unsolicited, always include a self-addressed, stamped envelope (SASE) for return of your material.

Business Letters

Business Letters

• • •

By now you may be saying to yourself, "So many things to know!" If so, don't despair. The business letter is an easy, if necessary, skill to learn. The sooner you master it, the sooner you can begin dealing with the commercial world of publishing.

Trends come and go, fancy paper, elaborate letterhead, intricate typefaces. But a business letter must meet certain standards, if you want to communicate effectively. The points that follow are of equal importance.

1) Put relevant ideas in the best possible order.
2) Say everything in the fewest possible words.
3) Convey your exact meaning.
4) Use conversational language.
5) Be courteous.
6) Use positive words. Exclude negative words.
7) Use vivid, "picture-provoking" nouns.
8) Write in the active voice, with specific action verbs.
9) Make it personal.

Some tips that apply to writing queries, cover letters, proposals, etc.:

1) Use good quality, <u>white</u>, 8 1/2-by-11 paper and black serif type.
2) Text must be creative.
3) Get to the point. Time is money.
4) Use all letters as selling tools for yourself and your writing.
5) Include a bio, if appropriate. See an example on page 164.

As a general rule, single space all business letters. There are no exceptions to this, unless an editor asks you specifically for a double-spaced letter. A rare request; it's happened to me only once.

By far the most popular business letter structure is the block form which makes typing easier and faster. Some use the indented block. Both have a single blank line between paragraphs. In the example on the next page, you see the indented block. A ¶ (paragraph marker) shows the approximate number of single lines to put between groups of information.

The first sample letter gives instructions. For specific types of letters, check the index or table of contents to locate the appropriate section of *Every Page Perfect*. You'll find many letters throughout.

The second example is of a confirmation letter to an editor of short nonfiction. A confirmation letter is used when an editor has accepted a piece of work or given you an assignment over the telephone, and you have no written contract for the piece. This letter insures that there are no misunderstandings and that you will get paid for the work you've done.

And finally, a sample letter using letterhead.

Remaining samples, in this section, are of the correct layout of the verification postcard and an envelope that's properly addressed.

Author's Name
Author's Address
City, State Zip Code
¶
¶
Date
¶
¶
Editor's Name and Title
Publishing Company or Publication Name
Address
City, State Zip Code
¶
¶
Dear Ms./Mr. Editor's Last Name:
¶

Place your name address, city, state, and zip code in the upper left corner. Leave two single blank lines above and below the date, then type the name and address of the person and/or company to which you're writing. Drop two more blank lines and type the greeting. Leave one single blank line before the body of the letter and between each paragraph.
¶

This is the indented block form for business letters. Indent the first line of every paragraph about one-half inch (10 to 12 spaces) from the left margin. Margins are 1 1/4 inches all the way around.
¶

Leave one or two single blank lines between the last line of the letter and the closing. There should be four or five single blank lines between the closing and your name. Type your daytime phone number and e-mail address below your typed name. Be sure to sign the letter.
¶
¶
Sincerely,
¶
¶
¶
¶
Your Name
Daytime Phone Number
E-mail Address

Author's Name
Author's Address
City, State Zip Code

Date

Editor's Name and Title
Publishing Company or Publication Name
Address
City, State Zip Code

Dear Ms./Mr. Editor's Last Name:

Thank you for your phone call this morning and for accepting "Fun With Clay" for publication in Hightime magazine. Be assured that I will be happy to make all the changes and additions you've suggested. With this letter, I want to confirm the details of our conversation and your instructions.

You asked me to obtain a release and waiver from Mr. Ed James for the use of his photograph of the clay baskets. I am to rewrite paragraph four, on page 2, to include an elementary school art teacher's opinion about using finger paints on clay, and add another anecdote, before paragraph six, on page 2. The finished article is to be about 1,000 words long, completed and mailed by August 17th, 2003. Hightime is buying First Serial Rights.

I understand that a check for $250.00 will be sent to me, at the address above, within five days of your acceptance of the revised and finished article.

If you agree with my understanding of our telephone conversation, please sign and date the enclosed copy of this letter and return it to me in the self-address, stamped envelope provided.

Thank you again for your acceptance of my article.

Sincerely,

____
Editor's Name and Title

Author's Name
Daytime Phone Number
E-mail Address

____
Date

Penny Quill
Postal Route 39, Summary, South Dakota 00000
(555) 555-5555 • PeQu@xxx.com

14 July 2002

Ardeth Werker, Senior Editor
Figtale Publications, Inc.
75468 River Avenue NW
New York, NY 00000

Dear Ardeth:

Your last letter made me so happy. You always manage to come up with exactly the right idea at the right time for me. How do you do it?

I've rewritten both Chapter Three and Four, of WALK TO THE MOON, with your excellent suggestions in mind. The heroine is now "on stage" most of the time and the villain is holding her hand every chance he gets. Hope you like what I've done. And if you don't . . . I'll do it again!

My next partial manuscript will be in the mail to you by October 22nd. You'll be glad to know that this one is a murder mystery with lots of scary characters and a triple measure of red herrings.

Take care and thanks again for the helpful letter.

Sincerely,

Penny Quill
(555) 555-5555
PeQu@xxx.com

Enclosure: Manuscript of WALK TO THE MOON

Verification Postcard •

Anytime you feel the need to know if your work has arrived safely on an editor's desk, it is perfectly proper to enclose a self-addressed and stamped postcard with your submission. Very little needs to be said in the postcard message.

As the sample below illustrates, a few typed or handwritten words on the message side of a standard postcard are sufficient. In the peace-of-mind department, so little time, postage, and effort can do so much!

In your cover letter, ask the editor to sign, date, and return your verification postcard on the day he or she receives your manuscript. Editors look for and expect this professional addition to your submission package and gladly comply with your wishes.

If your postcard is handwritten, neatly draw signature and date lines with a ruler and label them as such. The title of your submission can be either handwritten on a line or typed in. Your choice. If you prepare several of these postcards ahead of time, make them generic by leaving the work title line blank, then filling it in later for each separate submission. Make the cards less generic and more personal by preparing them individually for each specific title and using the editor's actual name and title beneath the signature line.

To: Author's name

Re: Work titled ______________________

Your manuscript has arrived safely at Figtale Publications.

____

Signature *or* editor's name (spelled correctly!) and title

____

Date

Thank you!

• Properly Addressed Envelope

Type your name and address, single spaced, in the left corner. Begin the addressee's address in the approximate center of the envelope and single space. Be sure to include an editor's title and the proper zip code.

This sample is not shown at actual business-envelope size.

Penny Quill
Postal Route 39
Summary, South Dakota 00000

Ardeth Werker, Senior Editor
Figtale Publications, Inc.
75468 River Avenue NE
New York, NY 00000

> [The writer] must teach himself that the basest of all things is to be afraid; and, teaching himself that, forget it forever, leaving no room in his workshop for anything but the old verities and truths of the heart, the old universal truths lacking which any story is ephemeral and doomed—love and honor and pity and pride and compassion and sacrifice.
>
> William Faulkner
> 1897-1962

The Business of Rights •

Author's Rights: A Selected List

1. Mass-market paperback book (including textbook, revised, & limited edition)
2. Hardcover book (including textbook, revised, and limited edition)
3. Trade-paperback book (including textbook, revised, and limited edition)
4. Digest use
5. Abridgment use
6. Condensation use
7. Selection use
8. Anthology use
9. Quotation use
10. Book club use
11. Reprint-edition use through another publisher
12. First- and second-serialization use
13. Syndication use
14. Advertising use
15. Novelty use (merchandising; toys, games, etc.)
16. Commercial use of the Work or material based on the Work
17. Motion-picture and tie-in edition use
18. Dramatic adaptation use
19. Radio use
20. Television use
21. Audio-mechanical and recording use
22. Audiovisual-mechanical and recording use
23. Electronic information storage and retrieval systems use
24. Xerography and photocopying use
25. Videocassette use
26. Large-print use
27. Foreign language translations
28. Braille transcription for the visually handicapped
29. Photographing, recording, and microfilming for the physically handicapped
30. Sublicense or sale of rights
31. Any other rights now existing or that may hereinafter come into existence

These and others (See pages 2 and 18) are the rights owned by the writer/author and protected by federal copyright law for all published or unpublished " . . . original works of authorship fixed in any tangible medium of expression from which they can be perceived, reproduced or otherwise communicated. . . . " These rights may be licensed, sold, optioned, willed, assigned, or given to others. If licensed, the contract should contain a time-limited Reversion of Rights clause and also reserve, for the author, all rights *not* granted. Options, too, should be time limited.

Always make sure that your business letters, confirmation letters, short-work submissions, and book contracts clearly state which rights are being sold, optioned, or licensed to the publisher.

Book-Length Fiction

Manuscript Form: A Novel Explanation

• • •

The first and most important lesson to be learned about manuscript preparation is the absolute necessity that the manuscript look neat and clean. Beyond neat and clean, there are so many things to know and remember, it is essential to have a manual like *Every Page Perfect* at hand. In this fifth part, Book-Length Fiction, we deal exclusively with the novel format and the protocol for the various ways a writer will be submitting a novel-length piece of fiction.

Notice that the examples in this book have been typeset in a fashion similar to what editors want to see when they open a writer's manuscript package. The typeface (or font, as it's referred to in computer talk) you're reading right now is called New Century Schoolbook, installed on a Power Mac G4 computer. To print copy, I use a Hewlett Packard LaserJet 4 ML. New Century Schoolbook is used throughout *Every Page Perfect.*

Before buying, borrowing, or renting a typewriter, word processor, or computer, make sure one of the typefaces or fonts supplied or purchased conform to a rounded, serif-type, easy-to-read pica-style and size, which gives you from 10 to 12 characters per inch. The example below shows the difference between a serif typeface and a sans serif typeface.

Serif (New Century Schoolbook) — Sans Serif (Helvetica)

In summary, there are only three facts to remember at this point: Editors have tired eyes. Use pica type or a 12-point font. Avoid elite type and point sizes under twelve. A note: Some standard computer fonts, like "Times" and "Times New Roman" should be used at the 14-point size. Take a look at the font comparisons below. Compared to 12-point Times New Roman face, the same font, at 14 points, is obviously easier on the eyes.

Times NR Twelve — Times NR Fourteen

Tired eyes always prefer double spacing, but there are other reasons for all that empty space in a manuscript. Editors and copyeditors edit by writing in the space between text lines and in the margins. Logically, they want room in which to do their eye-tiring work. Hence, the double spacing and generous margins are your own special gift to the person with whom you want to become a partner in a close and lasting working relationship. Always open your doors wide to opportunity with this special gift of space.

Every instruction on every page of this book has a purpose. Take the KEY WORD from the title in the header, for instance. If practically every editor in New York has rejected a particular book, the author may want to change the title before sending it out again (in disguise, if you will). Then, a key word on every page becomes a problem. A gallon of white stuff and a passel of time may force the decision never to use the KEY WORD in the header again—until two manuscripts wind up in the same mailer. If the mailer's tab accidentally gets pulled, in the wrong place at the wrong time, the editor may receive six hundred pages jumbled thoughtfully into a large sack by the conscientious postal employee who had to pick them up from the mailroom floor. You can guess the rest. (Yes, it happened to me.) Some editors will grab top-of-the-stack pages to read at home. Need I say more?

Some reasons for the particulars of formatting aren't so obvious at first; some may even seem arbitrary. They range from what an editor is used to seeing, to what a typesetting fitter must see. But it's guaranteed, if you follow the guidelines in this book, you'll never stray from what your editor *loves* to see in a manuscript presentation.

There's considerable debate regarding manuscript preparation. By all means, remember neat and clean. If you feel you must deviate from the format set out here for book-length fiction, please err on the side of kindness. More white space! Larger type!

To be on the safe side of the argument and end the margin debate for all time, let's give editors exactly what they want: *Every Page Perfect.*

I'll complete this novel discussion of novel manuscript form at the beginning, with an explanation of what should appear on your cover sheet, or title page, as it's sometimes called. (By definition a "title page" is the page in the front of a bound book that gives the title, author, publisher, etc.; therefore, we use the term "cover sheet" when talking about manuscripts.)

Every submission of long fiction should have a cover sheet. It not only serves as an attractive divider between the cover letter and the actual manuscript, but also contains some vital information. Your cover sheet shows such things as who wrote the manuscript, where he or she lives, and how to reach that person by telephone and e-mail. It also tells editors, immediately, whether they have the right manuscript on the desk, or whether it belongs down the hall in someone else's office. The sample on the next page shows where your choice of information goes.

There are three distinct sections on a cover sheet. The upper left corner is for the author's name, address, phone number, e-mail, and social security number. The lower right corner is for the copyright notice. Use the word "Copyright" *or* the © symbol (sample shows both). Update to the current year when necessary. (See 'copyright notice,' in the glossary for update info.) The double-spaced middle section of the page is for everything else. Title, by, and author's name are always a must in this middle section, along with other pertinent information. You, the author, must *choose the appropriate items* that will tell the editor or agent what's enclosed.

(Working Title), beneath the TITLE, tells the editor that you're still thinking and open to suggestions about the title. Use w/a (writing as), beneath your name, if you want to publish the book under the pseudonym stated. Proposal for . . . indicates that a short synopsis or outline is enclosed. (Chapter One through Chapter Three) tells that the manuscript is a partial. (Synopsis, Chapter One through Chapter Twenty) means that this is the second part of a partial manuscript submission.

No matter which descriptive items belong in this middle section of your cover sheet, center headings both vertically and horizontally on the page, as in the sample on page 50. Bottom line here? Make it look neat.

Avery Writer w/a A. N. Auther
Box AAA
Muse, Montana 00000
(555) 555-5555 - AvWr@xxx.com
SS# 000-00-0000

GONE WITH THE ZEN

(working title)

by

Avery Writer

w/a A. N. Auther

Proposal for the Philosophical Fiction Line

(Chapter One through Chapter Three)

(Synopsis, Chapter One through Chapter Thirty)

Proposal for a Series of Novels

Book One of the ZEN Series

Unless otherwise advised, such as by talking to an editor or agent at a conference, a query letter is most always your initial line of communication about an idea. There are four good reasons for this letter. First, it's a perfect short-sweet introduction. Second, editors don't have much time. Third, professional writers are in the writing business and a good query is good business. Fourth, a good query can keep you out of the slush pile.

Think of a query letter as a first meeting. Prepare it carefully, as if you were dressing yourself for your first date—beautifully clean, charming without cuteness, and flawlessly styled. This is the first time editors or agents will "see" you. Make them want to learn more about you and hear from you again by using vibrant verbs and sparkling nouns. Make them want to see you again by sending a short-and-to-the-point, immaculately groomed, perfect page. *Never* send a query letter out with strikeovers, words crossed through, handwritten margin notations or insertions, small type, or misspellings. Use only 8 1/2-by-11-inch, good quality, white paper, and a business-size envelope.

"Ideas are a dime a dozen." You've heard that before, and it's true, especially for professional writers. Thus, the second good reason for the query. Editors are pressed for time. In between meetings and conferences and countless demands from different departments, an editor must find a book with a new idea—one they haven't seen over and over again. Wouldn't you like to know, in a few weeks, if an editor is interested or not, instead of waiting for months until an editor has the time to read an unsolicited submission? Find out, up front, whether he or she has just bought or published a similar idea, or just simply hates the idea. A well-written query letter saves everyone a big chunk of time—and money.

The business of writing is just that: A business. You are a sole proprietor, in business to create and market a top-quality product. Just as you wouldn't consider stopping by to visit an acquaintance without calling first, don't consider trying to sell your manuscript to a perfect stranger, without getting in touch first and explaining what it's all about or finding out what the editor wants. Economics play a part, too. I mentioned savings in the paragraph above. A query letter costs the price of a postage stamp. A manuscript, its accompanying materials, return postage, and packaging, can cost a bundle to transport via first-class mail. (Note: Everything you send to an editor or agent should be sent by first-class mail through the United States Postal Service. Unless instructed otherwise by an editor, do not send a manuscript by overnight mail or by any other special delivery service. Every perfect page should *always* go first class.)

Finally, an "I'd like to see more" from an editor brings your novel idea out of the realm of back-room, some-day slush and up to the status of a read-this-first, solicited manuscript. Can you think of a better value for the few cents it costs to buy a stamp? Need I say more about the importance of the well-written query letter?

Author's Name
Address
City, State Zip Code

Date

Editor's Name, Title
Publishing Company
Address
City, State, Zip Code

Dear Ms./Mr. Last Name:

The query letter to an editor you've never met in person, or over the telephone, should show your best writing and include a very brief synopsis. If you wrote to this editor asking for guidelines and/or publisher's catalogue, your first paragraph could begin: Thank you very much for sending . . . I found the . . . very helpful. . . . You would then propose submitting a novel titled (TITLE IN ALL CAPS) for the category, genre, or imprint the editor purchases. Next, introduce your main character, hero or heroine, and his or her main goal with dynamic clarity. In other words, begin the short synopsis with the hook, that exciting, life-changing action which inexorably propels the protagonist into the adventure that follows. Imagine that you're writing the cover blurb for your novel. Read and study many jacket-flap and cover blurbs for guidance. Use action verbs and vivid nouns to describe characters in exciting fashion. Character goals must be well motivated, by background and present circumstances, and concern the character's most vital interest.

In the second paragraph, introduce the second major character (the villain or the romantic interest, perhaps). Again, describe this character's most important goal and the motivation behind it. Remember, if it's not worth fighting for, it's not worth writing about.

The main conflict in the book must be explained next and involve the characters introduced above. Action is the key to the descriptive prose needed in these two to four concise sentences. Bring the villain (antagonist) on stage here if you haven't already done so.

Keep the plot summary as short as possible, one paragraph should do the job nicely. Build to the climax, the ultimate crisis, then describe the resolution of that crisis. Remember, ultimate crisis means blackest moment, victory or shame, life or death! Remember, also: The query letter should never be longer than two pages. One page is best.

A note: Some time-saving research can be done in advance. Depending on current market conditions, some editors want to see a completed manuscript first, while others prefer a query, proposal, or partial. Find this information in trade periodicals and books or call and ask. Knowing beforehand that an editor wants a finished manuscript, after approving a queried idea, the writer can better project schedules and properly manage the time needed to comply with an editor's request. Best advice: Finish and polish your *first* novel *before* you query.

The final paragraph of your letter contains specifics. Tell the editor the approximate number of words in the finished work, making sure that your word count corresponds to the length of the books the editor is buying. This information is often available from the publisher in the form of guidelines. Estimate, as accurately as possible, the dates for completion of a full manuscript. Then add a brief summary of your credits. If you have them, use published novel credits for querying novel ideas.

But credits need not always be publishing credits. Mention any education, vocation, avocation, expertise, or experience that contributes to your ability to write the book. If you are acquainted with a famous (or fairly famous) person who writes in the same genre or is an expert in the field with which your book deals, and that person is willing to read your book and give you a quote, say so here. Nice words, from well-known people, make wonderful cover endorsements and can increase sales. The editor will be impressed and even more likely to ask for a manuscript. In this paragraph, you will also say something like this: "Be assured, I will abide by any editorial suggestions or changes you'd care to make." Then say thank you.

Again remember, editors read constantly, day and night, weekdays and weekends. Be kind. Use pica type or a 12-point font size on white, twenty-pound bond or good quality copy or laser printer paper. Margins are 1 1/4 inches all the way around the text. Get to the point! This is a business letter. Do not tell the editor what the cover art should be, that your book will sell a million copies, or how much your friends and family loved it. Never compare yourself to a famous author, or your book to a past or current bestseller. A one-page letter is ideal. Two pages is the absolute maximum.

NOTE: No guidelines available for the imprint or line you're targeting? Read and study books released by the publisher that are similar to yours.

Sincerely,

Author's Name
Daytime Phone Number
E-mail Address

Author's Name
Address
City, State Zip Code

Date

Agent's Name
Agency Name
Address
City, State Zip Code

Dear Ms./Mr. Last Name:

The query to an unknown agent differs from the query to an unknown editor in that you put your credits in the first paragraph. You've heard the well-known "Catch-22" paradox: If you've never published, you can't get an agent; if you're published, you don't need an agent. Neither is true.

Therefore, it's best to toot your horn first, then sell your idea. Either list your publishing credits, or tell why you are the person who is peerlessly qualified to write about your subject. There's a two-sentence maximum here and a mandatory appearance of the title of your book in ALL CAPS.

The rest of the letter is written in the same fashion as the letter to the unknown editor. Introduce your main characters and their goals with the hook, explain the problem, give a thumbnail synopsis of the plot, and sum up the solution to the final problem. End with manuscript specifics, an assurance that you will comply with recommendations, and a thank you.

Sincerely,

Author's Name
Daytime Phone Number
E-mail Address

Author's Name
Address
City, State Zip Code

Date

Editor's Name and Title, or Agent's Name
Publishing Company or Agency
Address
City, State Zip Code

Dear First Name:

Querying a person you know varies from the standard query letter. Since you already share something with this person, be it a simple phone conversation, a discussion at a conference, or an ongoing professional relationship, you can begin your query in a more conversational style. The first paragraph will be short, the subject personal. {Enjoyed talking to you on the phone this morning. . . . I'm so glad you approved of the revisions on the last chapter of. . . . }

Business matters can also be part of your brief first paragraph. A question about a royalty statement, the amount of an advance, or the receipt of a manuscript is perfectly appropriate. A more detailed business discussion should be sent in a separate letter.

The second paragraph clearly states the purpose of your letter. {I've just finished outlining an idea for your male adventure line. The completed manuscript will be approximately 75,000 words long and deal with the current Arms-for-Zombies problem in Northern Zoohala. I'll be happy to send you a partial manuscript immediately. The full manuscript will be ready in about two months.}

Your hook, character introduction, and story begin in paragraph three. See pages 52 and 53. End with the usual thank you and another chatty aside, if you think it's appropriate and doesn't detract from the story.

Sincerely,

Author's Name
Daytime Phone Number
E-mail Address

Section Two: The Proposal

• • •

Let's get a few terms straight from the beginning. For the purposes of our discussion here, a Proposal for fiction is the presentation of a novel idea in either outline or synopsis fashion. It is from two to six pages long, sometimes as long as twenty pages, but rarely more than this. Editors, who solicit proposals, will be glad to tell you what they want. The information is only a phone call or letter away. A novel proposal contains no sample chapters and is submitted, instead of a query letter, *only* when an editor asks for it. ('Proposal' also refers to a nonfiction submission. See page 113.)

By contrast, a Partial Manuscript submission contains several sample chapters, usually three, and a more lengthy synopsis or outline of the novel plot. The Partial Manuscript Presentation is covered in Section Three: Book-Length Fiction, starting on page 64.

Please be aware that some writers, agents, and editors use these two terms, proposal and partial, interchangeably. Others reverse their meaning. Still others have different names for either or both. Some ask for a partial when they really want a proposal and visa versa. It's confusing for the writer, but a problem easy to solve. Send for guidelines, or write a letter, or pick up the phone to call the editor and ask.

Other terms often confused: Outline and synopsis. Willy-nilly, these forms are called synopsis or outline. Editors usually refer to both as simply "synopsis."

An outline is written chapter-by-chapter, major event by major event. The outline story is interrupted by references to chapter numbers, either within a sentence or at the beginning of the corresponding paragraph. Though it bears no resemblance to the numbered and lettered step outlines you did in tenth-grade English class, we call this form an outline.

A synopsis is written more like a generalized summary of the novel plot, without reference to chapter numbers, and reads like an exciting short story. This is the more difficult form and should be used only by those writers who are expert at writing short stories. If you're using the synopsis form and have short story publishing credits, feel free to mention them briefly in your cover letter.

Write both outline and synopsis in the **present tense**, in vibrant story fashion, with brilliant characterization interspersed. Remember: Address only the novel's major events and characters in your proposal.

A proposal is most often sent when an editor has specifically asked for one. Sometimes writers use the proposal when they are already familiar with an editor's or an agent's needs and believe the plot idea to be too involved to have justice done in the shorter query.

A cover letter always accompanies a proposal and explains why the idea, length, subject, and/or theme is correct and timely for the targeted publisher's list. Naturally, as a professional writer, you will research ahead of time and know these "whys" before you mail out your novel proposal. Read, read, read! bestsellers in your chosen market!

Author's Name
Address
City, State Zip Code

Date

Editor's Name and Title, or Agent's Name
Publisher or Agency
Address
City, State Zip Code

Dear Editor's or Agent's Name:

A cover letter accompanying a proposal can have many purposes. If you don't know the editor or agent to whom you're sending it, the letter will introduce you (with or without credits) and explain why you are the perfect writer to deal with the subject and characters involved in the novel. Whether you know this person or not, however, always send submissions to a specific person. Use his or her name and title. Spell the name correctly.

If you know the editor or agent, and he or she is already familiar with the kind of work you can do, all that's required is a "Hi there," and a brief description of the specifications of the manuscript, such as: ZOOHALA ZEALOTS is a male adventure, written for your Nacho Hotcho Line, and totaling about 75,000 words. The manuscript is completed and can be sent immediately. Of course, I will be happy to make any editorial changes you might want.

Note: If you have experience or a track record with the agent, editor, or book line, you might offer a partial manuscript at this time.

A thank-you sentence or paragraph ends the short cover letter. Always enclose a self-addressed, stamped business-size envelope (SASE) for their reply. If you want rejected materials returned to you, include the appropriate postage and a self-addressed envelope of the proper size.

Sincerely,

Author's Name
Daytime Phone Number
E-mail Address

Author's Full Legal Name
Address
City, State Zip Code
(Area Code) Phone Number
E-mail Address
Social Security Number

NOVEL TITLE

by

Author's Name

Proposal for DARK DEADLY SPACE Line

Copyright by Author's Name, Year

Author's Full Legal Name
Address
City, State Zip Code
(Area Code) Phone Number
E-mail Address
Social Security Number

About 75,000 words

NOVEL TITLE

by

Author's Name

Proposal for DARK DEADLY SPACE Line

The first page of a proposal begins with your name, address, phone number, e-mail address, and social security number. On the line with your name, indicate the approximate number of words you expect to have in the completed manuscript. Center the TITLE (all caps), follow with "by," then your name. Two double spaces below your name, type "Proposal for," then state the purpose, such as, "Proposal for a Science Fiction Series." There should be exactly seven lines of text on this first page. All four margins are

1 1/4 inches, or larger, all the way around the text.

Page Two (and every subsequent page of your proposal) begins with a running header, placed 1/2 inch from the top of the edge of the paper.

At the left margin, use ONE unique word from your title, typed in ALL CAPS. On the same line, but on the right side of the page, type your last name, a hyphen (-), then the page number. Margins for the header are 1 1/4 inches from the left and right edges of the paper.

The text begins 1 1/4 inches from the top edge of the paper. Right, left, and bottom margins are also 1 1/4 inches. Using pica or 12 to 14-point font, double spacing gives twenty-five (25) lines of text per page. Note: Page One has only seven text lines. Write them in your most exciting style.

The content of the outline proposal is, of course, up to you. However, there are some important first steps. As in a query letter; the hook first, then introduce your main characters. Instead of two or three sentences for the shorter query form, you're free to make your descriptions somewhat longer. Always include your characters' main goals and the rationale that motivates the characters toward those goals. Write in **present tense**.

The main conflict of the novel should be developed next, followed by a brief summary of the conflicts between the major characters and major villain(s) that lead to the final disaster. A note: Villains don't always have to be people. A hostile environment, malfunctioning equipment, terrifying weather, etc., can be villainous as well.

The remainder of the outline proposal should be a chapter-by-chapter, major-event-by-major-event summary of the novel plot. Write one or two paragraphs per chapter and one sentence per major event, using dialogue very sparingly or, preferably, not at all. If you do use a line or two of dialogue, be sure the lines are as important as the title, the first sentence of chapter one, and the premise of your entire book all rolled into one.

Keep to the outline form by stating the chapter number somewhere in the first paragraph that addresses that chapter. The reference can be simple: In Chapter One, Hank . . . Or more elaborate: Hank thinks the worst is over after the roof caves in, but, in Chapter Three, the ice storm . . .

Your outline proposal ends with a vivid description of the climax, the final disaster, and a brief summary of the resolution of all conflicts. Don't be tempted to end with a question such as: Will Hank discover that Harry is already in Panama enjoying the fruits of his illicit dealings with the Ipso Factos?

Editors want to know what's going to happen. Beginning writers, especially, take heed. Finding a satisfactory solution for each plot conflict is one of the most difficult of all writing tasks. Let the editor or agent know that you're capable of fashioning a disastrous crisis and decisive climax, a convincing resolution, and a rewarding denouement.

Again, outline proposals, used as vehicles for queries, are short, with five to six pages the usual maximum length. Stray from this standard for a particular line or imprint only on the advice of an editor or an agent.

After the last paragraph, type THE END two double spaces below the last line, in all capital letters, in the center of the page. When packaging your manuscript for mailing, do not bind it in any way. Enclose an SASE.

THE END

Avery Writer
w/a A. N. Auther
Box AAA
Muse, Montana 00000
(555) 555-5555
E-mail Address
SS# 000-00-0000

About 65,000 words

WHEN THE WIND BLOWS

by

Avery Writer

w/a A. N. Auther

Proposal for Déjà View Line

Lucy Eldridge pales, feels a split second of weakness, then grabs for the baseball bat propped against the closet door. She isn't about to let this scraggly midnight intruder, with his hand on her jewelry box, become the latest man to defeat her today. Fired from her job, ridiculed by a haughty replacement, and dismissed unceremoniously by a telephoning, cowardly boyfriend--all in the past few hours--Lucy is in no mood to be robbed.

"Mister, you're a dead man."

The idea in a short proposal is to get the editor's attention immediately. This can be done with action and by putting the main character in jeopardy in the seven lines on Page One.

Of course, this intruder is Edward Blake, the hero of our story, who has very good reasons for looking so scraggly and being in heroine Lucy's apartment with his hand on her jewelry box. We'll probably find out later that Edward, the locksmith, has bungled his secret love's surprise birthday gift and party. But we'll love him all the more for trying so hard to make Lucy's thirty-ninth her best celebration ever.

Write both synopses and outlines in the third person (usually preferred) or first person, **present tense**. Both should be from two to six pages long as a standard, with five or six the usual maximum length. Again, the synopsis proposal differs from the outline in two major ways (described on page 56). First, the synopsis is written in narrative or story form. Second, the story is uninterrupted by references to chapters.

Margins are 1 1/4 inches all the way around. Place the header, containing a KEY WORD from the title, your last name, and the page number 1/2 inch from the top edge of the paper. Note that Page One has no header and is not numbered. All subsequent pages are numbered.

After the last paragraph, double space twice, center and type:

THE END

Remember: Never bind your manuscript submissions in any way. Send loose pages only. Always enclose a self-addressed, stamped #10 envelope.
Remember: Two hyphens (--) mean that you want the typesetter to use an em-dash (—).

Section Three: Partial Manuscript Presentation

• • •

"Let me see some chapters."

Lovely lyrics to any writer's ears, unless, perhaps, you haven't written those chapters yet. You're on the mark as soon as the post office gobbles up your query letter or proposal. The next move: Get back to your typewriter or computer and GET READY. That means writing a partial manuscript.

Actually, on the assumption that any editor or agent in his right mind is going to love your brilliant new idea, you should have at least three chapters and a synopsis of the plot finished and polished before you hear the music: "Let me see some chapters."

Exception: If you already know that your chosen editor will want to see a full manuscript, wait until you've finished and polished the entire book before mailing your query letter. You *must* know the market.

Several tasks should be completed before your query goes into the mail. First, write extensive character sketches, including characters' goals, for all your major characters. Do brief character sketches for all minor characters. Next, decide on the time span of the book, then create a chapter-by-chapter time-line and/or calendar sheet. On the date-by-date calendar sheet or time-line, plug in all major events that impact on the characters and propel the story toward its conclusion. With this complete, write a concise sequence outline, about two sentences per major event, for the entire book. Write the first draft of the first three chapters. At this point, you're probably ready to query an editor or agent who wants a partial.

If you are a slow writer, get at least a second draft of your first three chapters down on paper before you send out your query or proposal. This strategy gives you plenty of time to refine the synopsis (sequence outline) of the remainder of the plot, rewrite and perfect the chapters, and adjust any problematic areas in the story before hearing from the lucky editor.

There's another good reason for having a partial nearly ready to send out. Once you've written that much of a story, you have a pretty good idea whether you're on the right track with the characters and the plot. When the partial is completed, you can put the idea aside and get on to the next world-shaking idea, without worrying about losing your way through a complicated plot after it's been sitting on the shelf for several weeks waiting for the right-minded editor or agent to answer your query.

Important to remember: Most fiction editors want to see the first three chapters of a novel. It is *very* unusual for a fiction editor to ask for non-consecutive chapters, so don't worry that you won't be ready for the go-ahead. Just make sure that you write a total of at least fifty to sixty pages for the three chapters.

The synopsis can be written in either outline or synopsis form and is usually from two to twenty pages long. Short is more difficult, but advisedly better. Follow guidelines, if available, for synopsis length.

Avery Writer
Box AAA
Muse, Montana 00000

31 January 2002

Ruth Read, Senior Editor
File Thirteen Publishing
Box XXX
New York, NY 00000

Dear Ms. Read:

Thank you so much for asking to see WHEN THE WIND BLOWS. I'm sending the three chapters and a synopsis of the plot you asked for in your letter dated January 24th.

In this package, you'll also find an SAS postcard (for verification of my manuscript's arrival), a pre-addressed mailing label, and return postage for the manuscript. If you will be so kind, please sign and date the postcard and mail it back, as my assurance that WHEN THE WIND BLOWS has reached your desk safely.

{The postcard should be typed, have a signature line and date line at the bottom, and say something to this effect: Your manuscript, titled . . . , has arrived safely at File Thirteen Publishing. See Part Four, page 44, for a sample verification postcard.}

Again, thank you for your interest in this work. Be assured that I will be most willing to make any editorial changes you might request.

Sincerely,

Avery Writer
Daytime Phone Number
AvWr@xxx.com

Avery Writer
w/a A. N. Auther
Box AAA
Muse, Montana 00000
(555) 555-5555
AvWr@xxx.com
SS# 000-00-0000

WHEN THE WIND BLOWS

by

Avery Writer

w/a A. N. Auther

(Chapter One through Chapter Three)

Avery Writer
w/a A. N. Auther
Box AAA
Muse, Montana 00000
(555) 555-5555
AvWr@xxx.com
SS# 000-00-0000

About 65,000 words

WHEN THE WIND BLOWS

by

Avery Writer

w/a A. N. Auther

Chapter One

A partial is identified on the cover sheet by the words "Chapter One through Chapter Three." When specifically requested, you might send more than three chapters. The cover sheet should reflect this. As with a proposal, your name, address, phone number, e-mail address, and social security number appear in the upper left corner. When using a line for a pseudonym, dateline, or chapter name, etc., move the TITLE, byline, and other heading items up. Only seven lines of text appear on this first page.

Page two of Chapter One begins with the running header that will appear on each consecutive page of the first three chapters. Place a KEY WORD from the title in all caps at the left margin. Your last name (in upper and lower case), a hyphen (-), and the page number are at the right margin. Type the header 1/2 inch below the top edge of the paper.

Text begins 1 1/4 inches from the top of the page. Right, left, and bottom margins are also 1 1/4 inches. Vary 1/8 to 1/4 inch wider if you wish.

A partial is sent in response to an editor's request, after she's seen a query letter or proposal. Occasionally, a partial should be sent instead of a query, proposal, or full manuscript. This is acceptable when your market research indicates that a certain editor is reading only chapters and synopses, when an editor says so at a writers' conference, or in a telephone conversation. Editor's requirements often vary and depend on the many aspects of the publishing business, such as the number of titles published per month, the number of manuscripts backlogged, and the financial state of the publisher. Moral: Stay tuned to your market by reading writers' magazines, visiting publishers' web sites, talking to other writers, and going to conferences, seminars, association meetings, and workshops.

An active writers' group, or its newsletter, can help keep you up to date with the market news. Don't be afraid to pick up the phone and call an editor if you're unsure of what to send. Remember, it is essential to send exactly what an editor wants to see, read, and buy.

The last page of Chapter Three (Four or Five, as the case may be) will end the first portion of your partial. However, no notation of "THE END" will appear on that page.

Avery Writer
w/a A. N. Auther
Box AAA
Muse, Montana 00000
(555) 555-5555
AvWr@xxx.com
SS# 000-00-0000

WHEN THE WIND BLOWS

by

Avery Writer

w/a A. N. Auther

Synopsis

(Chapter One through Chapter Fifteen)

Avery Writer
w/a A. N. Auther
Box AAA
Muse, Montana 00000
(555) 555-5555
AvWr@xxx.com
SS# 000-00-0000

About 65,000 words

WHEN THE WIND BLOWS

by

Avery Writer

w/a A. N. Auther

Synopsis

(Chapter One through Chapter Fifteen)

Synopses, for partial manuscript presentations, begin at the beginning, even though you're submitting the first three chapters, because the synopsis is also used by other departments, like art and sales. Write these first seven lines on page one in the most exciting way possible, since some editors sneak a peek at the synopsis before reading the chapters. End the first-three-chapter portion with a vivid description of the precarious situation in which you've left your main characters in Chapter Three. The remainder of the plot follows in either outline or synopsis form, with scene descriptions in the order they appear in the novel. Write in **present tense**.

Each major event or scene in your novel should be given two to three sentences of explanation. The editor is most interested in what action takes place, the characters involved in that action, and how events affect them.

Write one to two paragraphs for each of the remaining chapters. Just as in your novel, each chapter description in the synopsis should end with a cliffhanger, such as the hero being left on a mountain top during the worst blizzard since ought-six, or the heroine discovering that she has just made her first million on the sale of a revolutionary fish food. Remember, good news can be just as stressful as bad. Imagine that this particular heroine, believing she has created an unpalatable loser, has previously and facetiously pledged all her earnings to the Foundation for the Preservation of Overpopulated Guppy Tanks. Million dollar stress!

A reminder about outline and synopsis form: Somewhere in the first paragraph that describes a new chapter, a reference to the chapter number appears when you're using the outline form. The synopsis form is written like a short story and lacks chapter number references. If you are a beginning writer or sending material to an editor unfamiliar with your work, the outline form can be a valuable device when used to show that you have a good grasp of proper plotting and story pacing techniques.

Notice here, and on all example pages, the type is left justified, right ragged. Do not justify type both left and right. Increasing the size of margins by 1/8 to 1/4 inch larger is okay. Standard number of text lines on this and all following pages, except the first and last, is twenty-five.

Varying the number of lines from page to page is not acceptable procedure. Pagination controls, in most word processing programs, allow you to turn off 'widows' and 'orphans' and other commands such as 'keep lines together' and 'keep paragraphs together,' so you have complete control over manuscript appearance. Depending on your font choice, you can usually adjust line spacing for 25 lines per page. In Microsoft Word, using Times New Roman font at 14 points, I set Line spacing to 'at least' and At '24 pt' by choosing Paragraph under the Format menu and clicking the Indents and Spacing tab.

It is proper to end the synopsis of the remaining chapters with a question—if you then answer it. For example: Will John and Marcia be able to bring the fish food business back from the depths of certain ruin caused by Marcia's impetuous philanthropy?

But of course! John and Marcia have renewed determination—and a brand new fish food formula!

Note that the running header continues throughout the synopsis or outline portion of the partial presentation. Cover sheets are neither counted nor numbered. Page One of the synopsis has no running header or page number. Synopsis page numbering starts again. Do not number the pages of the synopsis consecutively with the chapters.

The words THE END should be centered and typed two double spaces below the last line of your text. Package your submission without binding of any kind. Enclose a self-addressed, stamped #10 envelope (SASE).

THE END

Section Four: Complete Manuscript Presentation

• • •

There are two occasions when you send a completed manuscript to an editor, one glorious, one laborious (with glory attached).

The first, glorious, is when you've signed a contract after having sold your idea on a query, proposal, or partial. A caveat: Don't relax. Make a few hundred phone calls to tell everyone the good news. Then take a deep breath and continue writing. Always remember that you've already estimated the time to completion and told the editor when to expect the finished manuscript. Do *not* miss that deadline! The only thing worse is to send a poorly written, unprofessional-looking manuscript.

The second occasion, laborious, is when an editor asks to see the entire book before considering a contract. There's a lot of glory here, too, though. By all means make those good-news phone calls. And even though you don't have a contract to spur you on, you're still under the gun to complete the book by the date you promised. Yes, promised. You may not have used that word in your query letter, but the date you gave is a pledge. Editors plan their lines months in advance and it's possible that yours has already been tentatively scheduled for a particular time slot, twenty-four, or more, months hence. Do *not* disappoint her! Do *not* get discouraged!

But yes, I did say twenty-four months. Due to the economics of the publishing business, editors have to think long term. Let's say that you finish the book in six months and mail it. Editor takes a couple of weeks to get to it, another week to read and evaluate. If revisions are necessary, she'll write a revision letter and send the whole package back to you for further work. You finish in a month. We're up to eight months now.

When the new manuscript arrives on her desk, figure another two months to re-evaluate. Now, at this point, let's say she calls and says a contract is in the mail, which you receive and sign. The editor then does a line edit: correcting grammar, dividing aerobic sentences into readable chunks, fixing plot problems. Plan *at least* two months. Standard procedure then is to send it back to you for the corrections. You promise three weeks. Counting transit time, we're at thirteen months elapsed time.

The line-edited version now goes to the copyeditor. Copyeditors double-check and correct errors of fact, style, and continuity. Figure another three to four weeks. Time gone by, fourteen months. You then follow the copyeditor's instructions and fix the problems. Fifteen months.

Sales department (strategy), art department (cover design pizzazz), promotion (world tour or bookmarks), publicity (news releases, reviews), typesetting (body design), galleys. Two to four months = nineteen months.

Back in your court. Writer corrects galley proof errors (galleys or page proofs are typeset book pages). Note: Never rewrite anything at this point! You'll be charged for changes. Eight months now to bookstores—fix the galley, strip in body pages, cover color separations, shoot signatures, burn plates, print, collate, gather, bind, pack, ship, distribute, publicize, shelve. Send out seven more new-book-idea queries! Autograph!

Author's Name
Address
City, State Zip Code

Date

Editor's Name, Title
Publishing Company
Address
City, State Zip Code

Dear Ms./Mr. Editor's Last Name:

Cover letters remind editors of what they've requested from you and describe what's in your package. If you spoke with the editor on the phone, about the manuscript you're enclosing, refer to that conversation. If the editor wrote to you requesting the book and certain items, mention that letter or send a photocopy of it along with your finished manuscript.

Keep the cover letter short and businesslike. It should *never* be more than one page long. Be sure the editor's name and full title appear in the inside address. Call the publisher if you're not sure of this information.

Single spacing is standard for business letters. Use easy-to-read pica or easy-to-read, serif computer font. Begin your address block 1 1/4 inches from the top and left edges of the paper. Use your own preferred business letter style. See examples of business letters in the Business Letters section, beginning on page 39. Neat, clean, and perfect is the bottom line. (Example on the next page.)

Again, assure the editor that you are willing to make any editorial changes he or she deems necessary. (Remember: Editors know more about their target audience than you do.)

Sincerely,

Author's Name
Daytime Phone Number
E-mail Address

G. A. Novill
47 Coldwater Walkup
Diction, Arkansas 00000

7 April 2004

Eddy Torick, Senior Editor
Topfloor Books, Inc.
303 Mastadon Ave.
New York, NY 00000

Dear Mr. Torick,

I know I'm a week ahead of schedule, but thought you'd want FRICTION PLACE as soon as I'd finished. As you requested, I've included: my vita; a 5x7-inch black-and-white glossy (recently taken); the completed art fact sheet; a map of the fictional Friction, Arkansas (and surrounding area); and a copy of the map artist's signed and dated release and waiver (identified as: RELEASE AND WAIVER OF RIGHTS #1, Friction Map).

The plot, from Chapter Eleven on, has been completely revised to your specifications. The character of Bessie has been taken out altogether. You were right. The book didn't need her.

Thank you for all your help with this novel. Hope it's profitable for both of us. Further changes are yours for the asking.

Sincerely,

G. A. Novill
(555) 555-5555
GaNo@xxx.com

Vita — Résumé — Biography •

A vita, résumé, or biography is requested if a brief write-up about the author is going to appear in the book or in the publicity for the book. The information will be used as a guide, when the editor and/or advertising department does the publicity write-up for the book, news releases, press kits, and/or advertising copy.

Many forms of vita, bio, and the résumé exist and are fully explained in several books and pamphlets. When the editor says, "Send me a bio," any one of these forms may be used, as long as you keep it brief and to the point. One page is ideal. Two pages is the absolute maximum.

Tailor the bio to fit the project. For instance: If your main character can fly an airplane, by all means mention your own private pilot's license and flying adventures. If there is dastardly demolition in the plot, include your own experience with dynamite, fuses, and caps. If your villain is an evil psychotherapist or psychopath, list your own Ph.D. in psychology.

Useful information heading divisions are: Education; Experience; Accomplishments (including publishing credits); and Honors. Also include; organizations you belong to, media contacts, local libraries and bookstores, endorsement contacts, etc. Your date of birth, marital status, children, etc., are not necessary, but can be added, if they lend credence to the experience needed to write this particular book.

It's a good idea to design a publicity bio sheet for your own personal use as a marketing tool before your book comes out. Mine is one page long and includes my publicity photo. (Sample on page 164.) This one page doesn't have to be elaborate, just neat and clean—and it's easy to make up.

First, design a model on a piece of typing paper. Decide how much room the picture should occupy and where it will be placed. Draw a rectangle in this position, then plan your text around it accordingly. Take a print of your publicity photograph to a print or graphics shop, tell them what size picture you need, and ask them to shoot a half tone with a one-hundred line screen. This type of half tone can be photocopied without the usual muddy, smudgy-looking effects you get with a photographic print.

Your name should be on line one. Your address and phone number should be on the last line at the bottom of the page. Use a new typewriter ribbon or printer cartridge so type will be dark, black, and crisp. After you've neatly typed or printed your copy on clean, white paper, attach the half-tone photo with a few touches of past-up adhesive (available in handy sticks in most any variety store or business supply). Now you're ready to make as many copies as you'll need (white only) to send out to newspapers, magazines, bookstores, libraries, schools, radio and television stations. For e-mail versions, save your scanned photo in JPEG or TIFF format.

From the moment you put your query letter in the mail, be ready to send out this bio information (with or without photo) on a moment's notice. It's also a good idea to get your publicity photo taken early on. (More about the photo on the next page.) Most important: Make your bio brief, beautiful, neat, and clean. The publicity bio, page 164, is a generic example of form.

• Publicity Photograph

Granted, it seems a little early to be thinking about publicizing a book that's not yet mailed to the editor who asked for it, but you really must. The day your editor calls and says, "Send me your publicity photo," is not the day to go scurrying around town looking for a photographer who can fit you into an already busy schedule. Worse, this is not the day to pull out the dusty 35mm and ask your nine-year-old to snap a few shots on the end of a many-months-old roll of color film.

Publicity photos should be carefully planned. *First*, choose a local photographer who specializes in portrait shots, whose work you admire and can afford. Tell him or her what you need (black and white, head and shoulders, clear focus is standard), when you need it, and that you want to buy the negatives. *Second*, pick out appropriate clothing, something flattering that you look and feel especially good in. Solid colors are a must. Long sleeves photograph well. *Third*, visit your barber or beautician. Make sure photo day is not a bad-hair day. *Fourth*, if you wear glasses, ask your optometrist to lend you a pair of empty frames just like your own. *Fifth*, look straight into the camera, fold your arms, and smile.

Take your time choosing the pose from the many on the contact sheet the photographer supplies. You'll be living with this mug shot for about three years—after which time you'll want to get another done. A standard 5x7-inch picture is a good size print to order, always usable, easily stored and mailed. (Depending on the camera, a 4x6 may be standard.) Keep half a dozen on hand. When mailing, assure that your photo arrives safely by using a photo mailer or by placing it between two pieces of sturdy cardboard in a manila envelope. Mark the mailer: Photo, Do Not Bend.

Most important to remember: Always use a good, black and white (color if requested) portrait photo taken by a professional photographer. Focus should be clear, not soft. Pose should be straight forward. Dress in solid colors only. Sharp contrast prints best. Get your hair done. Smile.

Art Facts •

Art facts are required by some publishers and not by others. Your editor will let you know what is needed by the art department for designing the cover. Since the cover artists don't always get a chance to read the manuscript before it becomes a book, certain information is vital for their guidance. The publisher will sometimes provide a form to fill out, so we'll deal here with what information you should be prepared to provide.

Generally, the art fact sheet will call for a physical description of the heroine, and/or hero, and/or villain. The artist wants to know: Hair color, style, length; height; weight; build; distinguishing marks or features; and the style in which they normally dress. Sometimes the form will have a space for a one- or two-sentence explanation of the main theme, the main conflict of the book, and/or the ultimate goals of the central character(s).

Descriptions of at least two scenes from the book, if not three or four, will be required. Three short summaries, from one to three paragraphs, should contain setting details, descriptions of the clothing worn by the characters involved, the exact positions the characters are in, and the circumstances surrounding the scene.

Choose these scenes carefully. The cover is the first selling point the reader sees about the book, so you want to pick out those images that most vividly show the theme, setting, and your characters in action.

Publishers that don't furnish art fact forms may still ask the writer for character descriptions and cover art ideas. While you're writing the book, jot down possibilities as you go, to save time, when the editor asks.

And while we're on the subject of art. . . . The form on the next page is used when the writer wants to use artwork (usually somewhere in the body of the book) that has been created by someone else. A Release and Waiver must be signed and dated by the artist or photographer who is releasing the piece(s) for publication and waiving the copyright he or she possesses for use in your particular published work. A copy of this, or a similar form, is always required by the publisher for drawings, paintings, computer-generated graphics, photographs, etc., that have not been created by the author or publisher's artist. Your publisher may supply the forms.

There are two other documents of which you need to be aware. The Permission and the Affidavit (pages 157 and 159). You will be required to supply the publisher with a permission form, when using any previously copyrighted material. Your editor can send you the particular type blank form your publisher uses. Write to the person or company owning the copyright and ask him or her to fill out the form, sign and date it, and return it to you. In turn, you will send a copy of the original to your editor.

The affidavit is used when you, the author, have hired someone else to do some sort of research for your book. It simply states what facts have been researched, how or from what source the facts were obtained, and a statement of guaranteed validity of all facts supplied. Obtain this form from your publisher or you or the researcher may write it in letter form. This affidavit must be signed and dated by the researcher and *notarized*.

RELEASE AND WAIVER OF RIGHTS # *Insert your control number and/or ID**

For valuable and adequate consideration received, I, the undersigned, do hereby release to: ______________________ (hereinafter known as the "Author")
Author's Name

the absolute and irrevocable, non-exclusive right to publish the following, in his/her work, tentatively entitled: *Title or working title of your work**

Description of items released: *(List specific identification of photos, artwork, recipes, or other non-published items furnished.)**

a) ______________________________

b) ______________________________

c) ______________________________

1) To copyright the same in the Author's own name or any other name that the Author might choose.

2) To use, re-use, publish the above-listed items in whole or in part, individually or in conjunction with other items, in any medium and for any purpose whatsoever, including, but not limited to, illustration, promotion, advertising, and trade, and

3) To use the undersigned's name in connection therewith, if the Author so chooses.

I, the undersigned, hereby release, discharge, and waive all claims and demands of, or in connection with, the use of the items listed above, including any and all claims of libel or invasion of privacy, relating directly or indirectly to the Author's use of these items in his/her work.

This authorization and release shall inure to the benefit of the legal licensees, representatives, and assigns of the Author as well as the persons for whom the artwork was done.

Credit in any resulting work should read as follows: ______________________

____

I have read the foregoing and fully understand the contents thereof.
*(If under 18 years of age, the signature of a parent or guardian is also required.)**

______________________________ ______________
Signature Date

______________________________ ______________
Signature of Parent or Guardian Date

____
(Print) Full Legal Name Street Address City State Zip Phone

* *Items in italics are instructions for information to be inserted.*

G. A. Novill
47 Coldwater Walkup
Diction, Arkansas 00000
(555) 555-5555
GaNo@xxx.com
SS# 000-00-0000

FRICTION PLACE

by

G. A. Novill

Dedication

For Aunt Hobarth, the one person who believed this book would get finished.

For Mrs. Lattice, the lady who said it would never get done, and thereby spurred me on to THE very END.

For 'B,' you know who you are and what you've pushed me to accomplish.

Dedication: This "thank you" is an optional part of the front matter in a fiction book. Include it now so that the fitter and typesetter can more accurately determine the number of pages in the finished book. Number front matter pages, with lower case Roman numerals, in a standard running header.

Epigraph: Inclusion of a relevant quote or inscription is, again, your option. Always name the author and quoted work. A signed and dated permission form is required if you use copyrighted material. Epigraphs may be used in the front matter and/or at the beginning of chapters. Number the front-matter page, in a running header, as you would the Dedication page. Example on page 129.

Contents: A Table of Contents is needed if your chapters have designated names (other than the numbered variety). All page numbers in the Table of Contents should correspond to manuscript page numbers. See page 130.

Foreword: Usually, in nonfiction books, the foreword is written by someone other than the author and is optional (and rare) in fiction. See page 134.

Preface: The author's remarks to the reader are also optional in fiction. You might tell the reader why you wrote the book, thank individuals or institutions for their help, or recognize a researcher. Format on page 136.

Acknowledgments: Use this form when those who helped you write the book are not given recognition elsewhere. See page 138.

Map •

A map is sent along with the full manuscript for several reasons. The first, of course, is when the editor asks for one. Good maps can be obtained from any Chamber of Commerce, Visitors' or Tourists' Center, or Embassy. Write a letter asking for prices of the various setting materials you require. In some cases, you will receive what you need free of charge. In other instances, prices will be quoted so that you can send a check or money order for the purchase. Costs are usually very reasonable.

When the setting is particularly obscure, the editor may want to further orient the reader by supplying a map as a guide. Knowing this in advance, the writer can avoid delays in publishing by supplying a map ahead of time.

If your setting is fictional, you should take the time to either mark an existing map appropriately or draw a simple picture that includes known landmarks in the area. In science fiction and fantasy, you might create an entirely new world or universe. Be prepared to furnish whatever the editor will need to satisfy the readers' curiosity about the place.

Another sort of "map" that you'll sometimes find useful is a mock blueprint. Suppose the fictional castle in your mystery has an elaborate labyrinth of tunnels beneath the structure. The labyrinth, designed by you in a particular way, is the murder weapon. The editor will probably decide that the reader will want to see it.

Equally as useful might be a street map of either a real or fictional town, the floor plan of a large home, mall, or office complex, mountain trails, back roads, the layout of ranch house and outbuildings.

Making *Every Page Perfect* is the first way to please an editor. Writing a good story is the second. It may seem like a lot of work, but sending necessary manuscript materials, including a useful map, is yet another way to impress. Good advice: Always go one step farther.

The map below is *not* meant to be an example—simply a reminder.

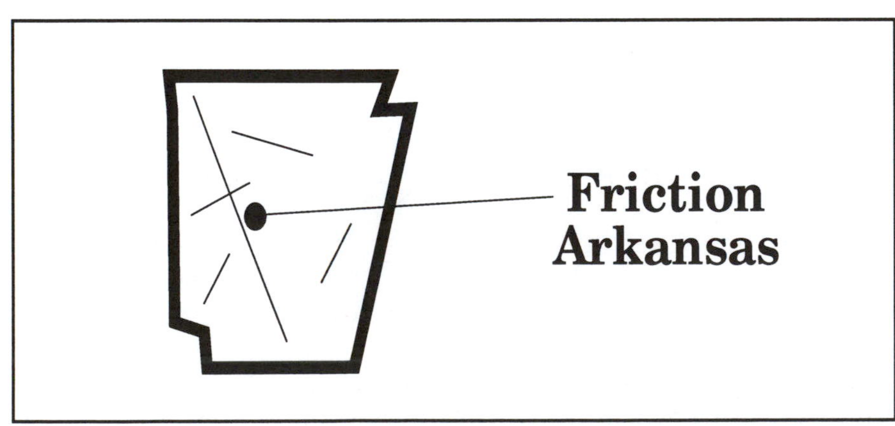

G. A. Novill
47 Coldwater Walkup
Diction, Arkansas 00000
(555) 555-5555
GaNo@xxx.com
SS# 000-00-0000

About 90,000 words

FRICTION PLACE

by

G. A. Novill

CHAPTER ONE

Top, bottom, left, and right margins are 1 1/4 inches wide. Double space text throughout. Your name and the word count go on the first line. Your address, phone number, e-mail address, and social security number follow. The novel title is horizontally centered on the page, typed in ALL CAPS. There should be seven lines of text on Page One. Place the heading lines accordingly. After your name, drop two double spaces for the chapter name or number, then two more double spaces and begin your text.

Beginning with Page Two, place a running header 1/2 inch from the top of the page. On the left, the title is shortened to one KEY WORD. Place your last name, a hyphen (-), and the page number on the right.

Begin the text 1 1/4 inches from the top edge of the paper. As on Page One, margins for this and all subsequent pages are 1 1/4 inches or larger. All pages of the novel should look like this page, unless they are the first or last pages of a chapter. Headers appear on every page but Page One.

Indent paragraphs 1/2 inch (10 to 12 spaces), continue to double space text lines. To leave a blank line in your text (noting a long passage of time or an abrupt scene change, for example) center either the proofreader's symbol (# # #), three asterisks (* * *), or three dots (• • •) on that line.

* * *

When sending a full manuscript that is not under contract, take time to find out what the publisher wants. Send for guidelines. Some fiction lines have stringent criteria about word count. A manuscript that doesn't meet a publisher's exact requirements will be rejected without a reading.

For an approximate word count of your book, count every word on five <u>full</u> manuscript pages, add totals, and divide by five. Multiply your answer by the number of manuscript pages, then round to the nearest hundred.

There are twenty-five lines on this page, standard format for all full manuscript pages. Using pica or 12 to 14-point type, proper margins, and double spacing, you'll have between 250 and 300 words per page. Adopt this standard format for everything you write and escape the tedious task of word counting for all time. Do not use computer generated word counts.

An example of the first page of Chapter Two follows.

CHAPTER TWO

The heading, CHAPTER TWO, should appear on the same line as the novel title did on Page One, Chapter One. If chapters also have a name, date, place, or other designation, begin the heading lines higher on the page. Notice that there are more lines of text on the first pages of following chapters than there are on Page One of Chapter One. No matter how many lines there are in the heading, always leave plenty of white space for the typesetter's notes on the first page of every chapter. The running header continues on a line 1/2 inch from the top edge of the paper.

All subsequent chapters begin with a page that looks similar to this one. Continue to number the pages sequentially. The only page of the manuscript proper that doesn't have a number is Page One of Chapter One.

The last page of your manuscript, or the last page of any chapter, does not necessarily have to have twenty-five lines on the page. The final page of the manuscript differs from all the rest, however, in that you must note that the story is finished. Do this by typing the words THE END two double spaces below the text in the center of the page.

* * *

A reminder: Unless otherwise instructed by an editor, underline those words you want typeset in *italics*. Even if you have the capability to italicize words, using your computer, don't do it. The typesetters are used to seeing and responding to an underlined word as they work. Keep them happy.

• • •

If your text for Chapter Last ends on line twenty-four, place THE END on line twenty-five. This is the only case where THE END appears one double space below the text. Under no circumstances send a last page that has only THE END typed at the top of the page. You may have to go back and revise slightly, pulling up a line to make room. You might decide to write another paragraph or two. Whatever works. Your decision.

# # #

Remember: Never bind novel manuscript pages in any way.

Note: Include a synopsis with a full manuscript submission.

Bottom line: Make Every Page Perfect.

THE END

• • •

Query Letter Submission •

1. #10 business-size envelope
   Addressed to a specific editor by name and title
   Return address
   Sufficient postage
2. #10 business-size envelope folded in thirds (for reply)
   Addressed to you
   Sufficient postage (pasted on the envelope)
3. Postcard with postage (optional)
   Addressed to you (for verification of query arrival)
4. Query letter (one page, two pages maximum)

Proposal Submission •

1. 9x12 manila envelope + mailing label (if desired)
   Addressed to a specific editor by name and title
   Return address
   Sufficient postage
2. 9x12 manila envelope (folded in half)
   Addressed to you
   Sufficient postage (paper-clipped to the cover letter)
3. Postcard with postage (optional, but recommended)
   Addressed to you (for verification of proposal arrival)
4. Cover letter (one page, signed, return postage paper-clipped to it)
5. Cover sheet
6. Proposal copy (outline or synopsis)

Partial Manuscript Submission •

1. 9x12 manila envelope + mailing label (if desired)
   Addressed to a specific editor by name and title
   Return address
   Sufficient postage
2. 9x12 manila envelope (folded in half)
   Addressed to you
   Sufficient postage (paper-clipped to the cover letter)
3. Postcard with postage
   Addressed to you (for verification of partial arrival)
4. Cover letter (one page, signed, return postage paper-clipped to it)
5. Cover sheet for the chapters
6. Chapter One through Chapter Three (or as requested by the editor)
7. Cover sheet for the outline or synopsis
8. Outline or synopsis

Complete Manuscript Submission •

1. 10x13 padded envelope or manuscript box + mailing label (optional)
   Addressed to a specific editor by name and title
   Return address
   Sufficient postage
2. Mailing label for return (if manuscript is not under contract)
   Addressed to you
   Paper-clip label to the cover letter
3. Proper postage for return (if manuscript is not under contract)
   Send international reply coupons (ICRs) for foreign publishers
   Paper-clip return postage to the cover letter
4. Postcard with postage
   Addressed to you (for verification of manuscript arrival)
5. 9x12 cardboard inserts (1 or 2 as required for photos, if included)
6. Cover letter (one page, signed, proper return postage and return mailing label paper-clipped to it)
7. Manuscript materials (as requested)
   Maps or other appropriate artwork
   Permissions (photocopies of forms that have been signed and dated by the copyright holder)
   Release and Waiver (photocopies of forms that have been signed and dated by the supplier of photos, facts, art, etc.)
   Affidavits (photocopies of forms that have been signed and dated by the source and notarized by a notary)
   Art facts (for cover design)
   Vita, bio, or résumé
   Photograph(s) (your publicity photo and/or setting photos)
8. Cover sheet
9. Dedication (if applicable)
10. Epigraph (if applicable)
11. Table of Contents (if applicable)
12. Foreword (if applicable)
13. Preface (if applicable)
14. Acknowledgments (if applicable)
15. Manuscript
16. Synopsis (if requested)

NOTE: From query to full manuscript, Book-Length Fiction submissions are seldom, if ever, submitted to Trade publishers by e-mail. For Web publishers, follow their guidelines for saving and transmitting text and photo files.

Book-Length Fiction: Series

Manuscript Form: A Serious Explanation

• • •

A series of novels, based on a collection of ongoing characters or a universally accepted premise (such as mystery or romance) is serious business to a publisher. It can mean large profits, or it can mean money down the drain if the new line never catches on. The decision to buy your novel series rests on many factors.

The questions a publisher asks about a series idea must be answered beforehand by you, the author. The order in which you address these questions doesn't matter. Most important is that you answer them all to the publisher's satisfaction.

Is the idea exciting, one that will sustain reader interest?

Is the subject timely now? Will it still be timely in five or ten years?

Does the subject encompass universal human feelings, failings, needs, and interests, and have a recognizable hook?

Are the ongoing characters fully developed?

Are the ongoing characters interesting, unique, and complex enough to sustain a multi-book appearance?

Is the setting (if ongoing) unusual or exotic or harsh enough to keep readers turning pages?

Is the readership national *and* international?

Is the reading audience large enough to make a profit?

Can the author deliver good writing?

Can the author deliver manuscripts on time?

Will the series be limited to a certain number of books (such as in a family saga or series limited by a particular historical event), or will the characters, situations, or settings support an indefinite number of books?

Can the author write enough books, in a short enough period of time, to launch the new line and keep it going through the first difficult months?

Will the series need other writers?

Are there other writers who have the expertise needed and who are willing to write other books for this line? (Your agent or a fellow writer may know the answer to this one, if you don't.)

Is the author willing to travel and make personal appearances, if necessary, for publicity and promotion?

Can the publisher afford to launch a new line? This question isn't an easy one to answer.

To find publishers who buy series ideas, look in the *Writers' Market*, under book publishers. Keep up to date with market news by reading *Writers' Digest, Publishers Weekly*, and other writers' publications. Other sources are writers, organization newsletters, conferences, and agents.

Finally, have you finished, at least, the first draft and a synopsis of the first book in your series, prepared character sketches, honed your premise into a brief, brilliant presentation, and sketched other stories?

When you've answered "yes" to all of the above, you're ready to approach an editor with your idea.

Imagine the Sherlock Holmes series of mystery stories without the hero, Sherlock Holmes. Impossible!

Why?

Complexity. Sherlock Holmes "lives" on the pages of his mysteries as surely as you are reading this book right now. The reason he can "live'" through so many stories is his intriguing and surprising intricacy.

Imagine Travis McGee without a crime to investigate. Impossible!

Why?

Tension. Without the danger to charismatic McGee's life and limb, the reader would probably stop reading halfway through Chapter One.

Imagine Parker's Spenser without a cause to fight for. Impossible!

Why?

Action. Without Spenser's "knightly" motivation to act and do the right thing, the plots of Parker's stories would die on page one.

Complexity, tension, action. Include them all in your query and/or proposal, done as a letter to the editor. It is necessarily longer than the brief queries sent out for a single book, since you have to establish not only sustained reader interest, several imaginative characters and plots, but marketing viability as well. Use the standard business letter form.

Create complexity in your characters by doing extensive character sketches before you begin writing. Along with all the necessary physical aspects of the characters, you'll need to define each person to a greater degree. Include: Education; avocation(s); vocation(s); family; flaws; moral or ethical faults; strengths; weaknesses; health status; psychological makeup; philosophy; and religious background. In each instance, define the characters' goals. Create motivation by writing a back story, a brief biography, if you will, for major characters. Describe events that left a mark, how the character reacted, and ultimately changed in response. Remember: If a character and his/her life goal and book goal aren't worth fighting for, they aren't worth caring or writing or reading about.

Tension results when heroes and heroines run into trouble, conflict, and disaster. Get your characters into a boiling cauldron, as soon as possible, by bringing a villain on stage to interfere with their admirable goals and put their lives in danger. The sooner conflict begins, the better.

Action is what happens when characters move or speak. Move characters toward their goals, then give them disasters to confront head on or detour around. Frustrated characters, in jeopardy, who figure their own way out of problems and continue moving toward worthwhile goals, despite the odds against them, are most interesting.

If you prefer, the query itself may be a short, one- or two-paragraph letter introducing you and your credits to the editor. The proposal would then be presented, with a cover sheet, in standard proposal format, using either outline or synopsis, as shown in Part Five, Section Two, beginning on page 56, of this book.

Author's Name
Address
City, State Zip Code

Date

Editor's Name, Title
Publishing Company
Address
City, State Zip Code

Dear Ms./Mr. Editor's Last Name:

Begin with a hook into the character, family, place, or situation that will be the uniting link for the series. This opening sentence must capture the imagination of the editor immediately. Continue by describing the unifying character or idea, with a focus on goals and motivations. You need not go into too much detail here. All you're trying to do is interest the editor in the basic premise. Exciting writing, that highlights action, will serve you best.

If you are developing a series around a character, he or she must be complex, noble enough to make the reader cheer, and flawed enough to keep him or her in hot water--and the reader wondering and caring.

A family that is the center of a series must consist of a variety of different and interesting characters, bound together by a common family goal, yet separated by personality, appearance, independent determination, and disparate (often conflicting) personal goals.

A location/setting must have the potential for drama. It must be a place that puts harsh demands, of one sort or another, on those who live there. It will be useful, when deciding on such a place, to remember the basic conflicts of: person against person; person against nature; person against himself; person against society; person against God; person against the supernatural; and person against machine. Any and all of these can be used to good advantage in a well-chosen setting.

A situation has to be complex enough, and the characters diverse enough, so that the various people confronted can approach the complicated predicament in vastly different ways. If there is only one way to respond to the ongoing situation, the books in the series will be too similar to hold readers' interest.

Describe the first novel in detail with, at least, four to five paragraphs devoted to the entire plot, characterization, climax, and resolution. Propose plot ideas for a few of the later novels. Do this in a sentence or two in your most glossy style. Imagine you're an editor with only a minute to read the idea for your series. Make each sentence sensational.

Explain, in one paragraph, why your idea will work for a series of books. Show that there's sufficient character motivation and growth possible to appeal to a wide audience and sustain no fewer than the number of novels you initially envision. Make it clear whether each book depends on the previous one for continuity (as in a family sage), or whether each book will stand alone with a few ongoing characters.

Mention the status of the series. (Before sending your query, have the first book, character sketches, premise explanation, brief outlines of two other books, and three or more thumbnail plot sketches completed.) Let the editor know that you can have these finished items in the return mail.

Once you've established the worth of the idea, the characters, the subject, setting, and major conflicts, it's time to address the other pressing questions involved with buying a series. Refer back to the explanation at the beginning of Part Six, page 90. Answer the remaining questions in any order that seems appropriate. Whenever possible, back up your claims for national and international readership and market share with statistics. You'll find information on the Internet or in several helpful books packed full of demographic, financial, and other such useful numbers in your library. The editor must know that your series idea will be a moneymaker.

If you are an author with previous novel publishing credits, don't hesitate to send a sample copy of your best book along with your letter. If you've never missed a contract deadline, be sure to say so. If you've been able to produce several books in a short period of time, let the editor know this, too. When giving your credentials, be sure to include any special expertise you have that specifically qualifies you to write your series.

Your query/proposal should be no longer than three pages. Single spacing is the norm. This is a business letter. Use all the sales and letter writing skills you can muster. Always address it to a specific editor by name and title, and let the editor know that you're willing to comply with any editorial changes that might be required.

Sincerely,

Author's Name
Daytime Phone Number
E-mail Address

Section Two: The Complete Manuscript Presentation

• • •

While similar to the novel presentation found on Pages 73-86, the series presentation has striking differences. Part One, character sketches and series premise. Part Two, complete manuscript for Book One. Part Three, synopses and thumbnails.

The character sketches are detailed descriptions of the significant, ongoing characters who will appear in every subsequent novel. If the series is to be an anthology, the character sketches can be omitted. In an anthology, each book stands alone. Rather than ongoing characters, the novels are unified by a device, such as; a timeless philosophical concept, a unique setting, or a universal ideology.

Polish your character sketches until they read like brief but exciting biographies. Detail every important aspect of every ongoing character, so that the editor will feel she wants to meet them in person. Shallow characters, who don't shine, don't sell, especially at this level of marketing. I can't stress enough the importance of extensive work on all of your major characters.

With the same care, the premise must be well thought out. Ideally, you should be able to state the premise in one sentence. Luckily, you can take up to two, double-spaced pages to explain the driving forces that propel the characters through your stories. This marketing tool, called the Novel Series Premise, shows that your theme is so universal, so intriguing, so all-encompassing and timeless that readership will be both vast and faithful.

Think of the series presentation as an elaborate extension of a query or proposal the editor has already seen. It expands on the ideas previously presented and shows your skill at weaving the threads of many concepts and varied characters into a cohesive whole.

A word of warning about the chapters you send. As with any other submission, these must be as perfect as you can make them. This is no time to mail out a first draft—or even a fifth. Rewrite and revise until Book One is honed to such a fine quality that you'd bet all your future royalties on it. To help you get onto the right track, right from the start, read books that you especially admire in a best-selling series similar to yours. Read books for which you'd pay hardcover prices. Read books by series authors you'd like to meet. Read a lot of them.

Future stories must be presented in an exciting, but capsulized form, to prove to the editor that you have thought well beyond the first book in your series, and are ready, able, and willing to write at least five more books. The synopsis of Book Two can be from two to six pages (or as requested). Synopses for Books Three, Four, and beyond will be one-paragraph to one-page-long thumbnails (or the length requested).

Each section of the presentation has its own explanatory cover sheet.

Of course, a brief cover letter accompanies your series manuscript presentation.

Lyza Morr
456 Lucius Ave.
Merlin, MO 00000

2 August 2004

Gwendolyn Wynne, Senior Editor
Artair Press
4 Marlon Way
New York, NY 00000

Dear Ms. Wynne:

Thank you for your interest in the proposed series, THE SILHOUETTE CUTTER, centering on Jacques Freneau, the elderly silhouette maker who is part artist, part seer, and part magician.

I'm sending a detailed character sketch of Freneau, further explanation of the overall series premise, the complete manuscript of Book One, a synopsis of Book Two, and thumbnails of Freneau's coming adventures.

A CUT ABOVE, the first book in THE SILHOUETTE CUTTER series, introduces Freneau as he is hired to cut silhouettes of the Williams family's children, only to find himself assisting a child unjustly accused of murder.

Also enclosed is a copy of your letter requesting this novel series submission.

Again, thank you for your interest in THE SILHOUETTE CUTTER. Be assured that I will make any editorial changes you find necessary.

I look forward to hearing from you at your earliest convenience.

Sincerely,

Lyza Morr
(555) 555-5555
LyMo@xxx.com

Lyza Morr
456 Lucius Ave.
Merlin, MO 00000
(555) 555-5555
LyMo@xxx.com
SS# 000-00-0000

THE SILHOUETTE CUTTER

by

Lyza Morr

Proposal for a Series of Novels

(Character Sketches and Series Premise)

CHARACTER SKETCH

The character sketches give detailed information about the hero, heroine, villain, and any other major characters who will appear in every book. The more complex the main characters, the more background and motivation you should show, up to a maximum of two pages per character. You will do a separate sketch for every character who is a vital part of the unifying series idea. Number these pages 1 of # in a running header.

Begin with the character's name and relevant background. Were there any experiences in his or her past that force the character to act in a particular way? Are any of the character's motivational fears or driving goals rooted in childhood trauma, guilt, or unhappiness? It isn't necessary to go into such detail that you tell the name of a long-dead puppy or pet cockatoo, unless those pets have a significant bearing on the stories. Keep the focus squarely on what motivates the character to act in the way he or she does. For instance, why does your detective like to sleuth?

Go next to the character's worthwhile goals. What does he or she strive for in the course of the first plot? What does he or she want to accomplish within the next year? Two years? Five years? If the character is to be the focal point of five or more novels, he or she must be complex enough to sustain interest. Give the reader concerns, not only with the character's approach to a specific plot's problems, but with all aspects of the character's life. To do this, create a character who is believable (flawed), unique (a talent perhaps), likable, and lovable. To carry a series, make characters' long-term goals admirable and worth striving for.

Include the character's personal information: Profession; personal relationships; hobbies; and successes, past or planned. Pertinent eccentricities, likes and dislikes, loves, hates, fears, and distinctive physical description should all be included.

A character sketch should read like a narrative rather than a résumé. Through a combination of action and reaction, show why the character thinks, feels, and behaves as he does throughout the series. In doing this, you will find yourself touching on future plots of one or more of the series novels. This is perfectly acceptable, and even necessary, although the most detailed plot description offered will appear in the synopsis of Book Two. The editor, however, will see more possibilities as they relate to the briefer thumbnail plot sketches you'll be sending.

Be selective in which characters and how many you choose to write sketches on. If you include too many, your series will begin to sound like an unfocused jumble, featuring a cast of indistinguishable thousands. Also, every page between the cover sheet and the actual start of Book One, Chapter One delays the editor from seeing your best work.

Adapt this character sketch form to suit the needs of your series. If requested, include a one-paragraph description of the lesser characters who will have a bearing on all the stories. (Do each on a separate sheet; number pages accordingly.) Perhaps you'll need to give background and details about an entire family. Whatever your logistics, the order in which character details are introduced is also flexible. However, once you've decided on a particular sequence, stick to it for all characters sketched.

Last word: Make your characters come alive.

NOVEL SERIES PREMISE

The novel series premise is where you must convince the editor that your idea requires a certain number of books. Solid reasoning is called for here so that the logical conclusion of the editor will be that your theme has a recurring, unifying subject. Number premise pages in a header one-half inch from the top of the edge of the paper, a KEY WORD from the series title on the left, Last Name, hyphen, and 1 of #, 2 of #, etc., on the right.

Describe the overriding conflict that carries through the proposed number of novels, such as a war, the attempt to capture a certain villain, or the desire to see justice done. Express this conflict in terms of the main character or characters' goals and motivations. There must be enough dramatic possibility to sustain the desired number of books. Remember Goldfinger in the *007* thrillers. Remember Sherlock Holmes' nemesis, Moriarty. Remember Donald Westlake's John Dortmunder and John's wish to stay "invisible" to the police, in spite of his friends' wild schemes.

Explain those motivations that will keep the series moving forward. What obstacles must be overcome that are so overwhelming they require more than one book? Why are the character's goals so important that the fight to reach them must continue?

What other problems might arise for the characters in this series? What are the characters' possibilities for growth? Be sure that major characters, featured throughout the series, do not grow and mature too much by the end of the first or second book. Too drastic a change in one plot may leave the character without room to grow in the next.

Tell what makes your series premise unique, and why you think it will have reader appeal. To do this, read other series books being published so you can point out important and ultimately salable likenesses, then the differences that favorably set your series apart from all the rest.

You will notice that much of the information contained in the premise has already been stated, to some degree, in the query/proposal and the character sketches. Don't worry about this. The purpose of the premise is to bring all the characters and possibilities together in one cohesive idea and to sell the editor on the viability of a multi-book project. The editor must be convinced that the series characters and the additional one-book characters and situations will create plot-focused, character-driven dramatic questions that keep readers reading, page after page. This premise should promise the possibility of extraordinary questions that imply countless challenges concerning the human situation.

A brief reminder of any time-sensitive marketing statistics, mentioned in your query, can be stated again if the characters and premise directly correlate to an immediate, real-life experience or news event.

The explanation of your premise should be brief, one or two pages, double spaced. Center the heading NOVEL SERIES PREMISE at the top of the page, 1 1/4 inches from the top edge of the paper. Drop two double spaces and begin the text. Margins for the text are 1 1/4 inches or larger left, right, top, and bottom.

Lyza Morr
456 Lucius Ave.
Merlin, MO 00000
(555) 555-5555
LyMo@xxx.com
SS# 000-00-0000

A CUT ABOVE

by

Lyza Morr

Book One in THE SILHOUETTE CUTTER Series

Lyza Morr
456 Lucius Ave.
Merlin, MO 00000
(555) 555-5555
LyMo@xxx.com
SS# 000-00-0000

About 70,000 words

A CUT ABOVE

by

Lyza Morr

Book One of THE SILHOUETTE CUTTER Series

CHAPTER ONE

Black on White

The first manuscript page of Book One of a series has your personal information in the upper left corner, word count on the right. Center TITLE and other heading lines to allow seven lines of text on this Page One. The number of the book and title of the series appear beneath the author's name, followed by the chapter number and chapter name (if any). Structure Page Two as you would for a single book presentation (example on page 68), with running header and twenty-five lines of text per page.

CHAPTER TWO

Shadows At Dawn

Type the heading CHAPTER TWO, in ALL CAPS, on a line in the approximate center of the page. The chapter name (if you're using one) is centered two double spaces below. A time, date, and/or place line would appear below the chapter name. Text begins two double spaces below the last heading. Ten to twelve lines of text are standard for all first pages of subsequent chapters, so adjust heading lines accordingly.

The running header, 1/2 inch from the top edge of the paper, which began on Page Two of Chapter One, continues throughout the rest of the book. A 70,000-word manuscript will be from 230 to 280 pages long, depending on the type and size of font or typeface used.

Lyza Morr
456 Lucius Ave.
Merlin, MO 00000
(555) 555-5555
LyMo@xxx.com
SS# 000-00-0000

FROM EVERY ANGLE

by

Lyza Morr

Book Two in THE SILHOUETTE CUTTER Series

Synopsis

Lyza Morr
456 Lucius Ave.
Merlin, MO 00000
(555) 555-5555
LyMo@xxx.com
SS# 000-00-0000

About 70,000 words

FROM EVERY ANGLE

by

Lyza Morr

Book Two in THE SILHOUETTE CUTTER Series

Synopsis

Another Page One. Again, no page number or running header. The TITLE is centered, heading lines are spaced so that seven lines of text appear here. In your most exciting style, capsulize Book Two in either synopsis or outline form (see page 56). End each chapter description with a can't-put-it-down cliffhanger. Write in present tense.

Start renumbering the synopsis, in the running header on Page Two, with the numeral 2 on the right. Continue with the KEY WORD from the title of Book Two (on the left). Note: Remember to divide Book One chapters and Book Two synopsis with a cover sheet.

The last page of your synopsis is the last page concerning Book Two, but it isn't the last page of your presentation. Depending on the number of books you're suggesting for your series, several thumbnail synopses will follow the synopsis of Book Two. {Note: It's possible the editor will ask for more than one full synopsis. If so, follow the editor's instructions and submit as many detailed synopses as requested.}

The thumbnails are done in much the same style as the query/proposal, explained on pages 91-93, except that these can be somewhat shorter, since the editor is well acquainted with the characters and the premise. A thumbnail sketch is simply an explanation of character, plot, and conflict presented on one page. Even one paragraph can do the trick for some ideas. If you can get the information down in an exciting way in a few sentences, so much the better. Do the remaining plot summaries, as many as you have in mind, in a few paragraphs. Usually, 200 words will be sufficient for these short sketches.

The thumbnails should have one cover sheet for the entire collection. Begin with the story TITLE (centered, in all caps) and end with THE END. Pages are numbered, in a header, in the same manner as the Character Sketches and Series Premise (1 of #, etc.). Examples of a one-page and a one-paragraph thumbnail follow. Remember: Write synopses and sketches in the **present tense**.

THE END

• Sample Cover Sheet for Thumbnails of Future Series Titles

Lyza Morr
456 Lucius Ave.
Merlin, MO 00000
(555) 555-5555
LyMo@xxx.com
SS# 000-00-0000

THE WOODWRIGHT'S DISGUISE

SHARP WIT

A SLICE OF LIFE

SHADOWS FROM THE PAST

by

Lyza Morr

(Thumbnail Sketches for THE SILHOUETTE CUTTER Series)

THE WOODWRIGHT'S DISGUISE

"I'm going to die right here in the woods--and I've never even tasted a kumquat!" Worse, in sixty years, Jeanetta Lotz has never seen a kumquat.

Lost, disoriented, her ankle badly injured, Jeanetta's cries go unheard by her fellow Hefty Hikers. Alone and disabled, she resigns herself to a dignified death among the ancient Illinois oaks--until the "kumquat" arrives. Knight in a bright orange shirt, hiking through the forest to his shop, Jacques Freneau, using the alias Marcus Louden (because he's been hired, by Jeanetta's jealous husband, to follow her), not only saves Jeanetta from a dignified death, but begins to light her way out of the dark woods of uncharacteristic depression and cynicism.

Just one week before, Jeanetta hadn't cared if she ever saw the light of another day, but the woodwright changes all that. Depression over a still-painful injury evaporates as Marcus gently, but firmly, insists on reviving physical therapy. Anti-social behavior, the vain indulgence that had gotten her lost from the other hikers in the first place, emerges, then disappears as the two share the warmth of the cheery woodwright's shop.

Once an enthusiastic expert with all manner of stitchery, Jeanetta must now be convinced that her disability is more in her imagination than in her injury. Her reintroduction into the world of productive labors becomes an exciting, romantic stroll with a magician of the heart, THE SILHOUETTE CUTTER. THE WOODWRIGHT'S DISGUISE is a story of patience, hard work, and the healing power of true love.

THE END

SHADOWS FROM THE PAST

The aged and gnarled Jacques Freneau confronts the black secrets of his own youth in the person of Percy Freneau, the son who abandoned him three decades before. Will the itinerant silhouette cutter and the all-too-respectable banker be able to reconcile their brooding hatred in time to stop the murder of Percy's fiancé, Hallies Blare? Ms. Blare, the only person who knows the secret of Jamesborough, Pennsylvania, also holds the key to Jacques' survival and Percy's escape from a perilous, clandestine life. She must, and does, become the silhouette cutter of destiny. Neither father nor son realize, until she forces a reconciliation, that Hallies can deftly wield the black and white, double-edged sword of both killing and healing words.

THE END

The paragraph above is an extremely short example, but contains all the elements necessary in a series thumbnail.

For each of the several additional novels proposed for your series, you will write up to one double-spaced page in the glossy style of a book cover blurb. Write the thumbnails in the third person, present tense, using vivid nouns and dynamic verbs.

As above, center the book TITLE and begin the story two blank lines below. Indent the text as usual. Margins remain the same, 1 1/4 inches or larger. Running header labels thumbnails as THE STORIES.

Introduce and describe the major supporting character(s) and his, her, or their relationship to the ongoing series character(s). Set up the main conflict(s) for the book, then briefly summarize the plot and principal dilemma. You may imply the resolution to the major crisis with a plot question or describe the catastrophe and denouement fully.

Notice that in this last sketch the ongoing character, Jacques Freneau, has aged quite a bit, possibly indicating that this is the last book in the series. From spry silhouette cutter in *A Cut Above*, to the energetic woodwright in *The Woodwright's Disguise*, Freneau now faces the ultimate crisis when his secret past and hateful son finally catch up to him.

NOTE: Write each thumbnail on a <u>separate sheet</u> of paper.

Section Three: Checklists

• • •

Query and Proposal •

1. 9x12 manila envelope + mailing label (if desired)
   Addressed to a specific editor by name and title
   Return address
   Sufficient postage
2. 9x12 manila envelope (folded in half)
   Addressed to you
   Sufficient postage (paper-clipped to the envelope)
3. Postcard with postage (see page 44)
   Addressed to you (for verification of query/proposal arrival)
4. Query letter or query/proposal
5. Cover sheet (for the proposal, if included separately)
6. Proposal (if included separately)

Complete Manuscript Presentation •

1. 9x12 padded envelope or manuscript box + mailing label (if desired)
   Addressed to a specific editor by name and title
   Return address
   Sufficient postage
2. Return mailing label (paper-clipped to the cover letter)
   Addressed to you
   Sufficient return postage (paper-clipped to the cover letter)
3. Postcard with postage (see page 44)
   Addressed to you (for verification of partial arrival)
4. Cover letter (return postage and mailing label attached)
5. Cover sheet for Character Sketches and Series Premise
6. Character Sketches
7. Series Premise
8. Cover sheet for Book One
9. Manuscript of Book One
10. Cover sheet for the Synopsis of Book Two
11. Synopsis of Book Two
12. Cover sheet for the Thumbnail Sketches
13. Thumbnail Sketches

NOTE: From query to full manuscript, Series Book-Length Fiction submissions are seldom, if ever, submitted to Trade publishers by e-mail. For Web publishers, follow their guidelines for saving and transmitting files.

Book-Length Nonfiction

Manuscript Form: A Factual Explanation

• • •

Putting together a book-length work of nonfiction is very much like juggling—if you're using fourteen balls . . . and they're all on fire.

The burning need for accuracy sets them aflame. A million bits of information keep the conflagration going.

First, of course, you must come up with a good idea. Second, you must discover an original slant or treatment of the idea. Third, you'll need to sell the idea to a publisher. Fourth, you're going to have to write the book.

Ideas are easy. They're everywhere. They come from things you've read, heard, seen, and experienced firsthand. Professional writers have so many ideas their offices fairly creak at the seams with file folders, index cards, drawers and boxes full of inspiration scribbled on everything from cocktail napkins to matchbook covers.

Book publishers want all kinds of nonfiction manuscripts that address everyday difficulties. They want to hear about better ways to cope, overcome problems, enjoy more rewarding relationships, travel, live, succeed, make money, invest, save, eat, diet, stay healthy, and be a better parent, to name just a few. True crime, biographies, and popular psychology seem always to be hot sellers. Cookbooks remain popular—and sell well, year after year—with enough categories to satisfy every interest, taste, test kitchen, and backyard grill.

The fresh angle can be much more difficult—but it's not even close to being an impossible task. Remember, the well-known fire-starter phrase in fiction writing is, "What if . . . ?" In nonfiction you might start out with a phrase such as, "Well, if it were up to me, I'd do it. . . . " Or, "I wish someone would. . . . " Or, "These tasks would be much easier if. . . . " You might also give some thought to *who* you know. Some of the best-selling stories of all time are the tales of a person's struggles to succeed through seemingly insurmountable odds. Maybe even your own!

Selling an idea to an editor is like jumping into a cauldron of boiling water. You're in the hot seat from the word go, and your facts and your logic (not to mention your writing) had better be flawless. If you say thirty-four million people are potential readers, have black-and-white statistics from a reputable source to back you up. If you say your no-fat soufflé is never-fail, make sure you've spent enough hours in the kitchen to prove it. If you say you can get a celebrity to pose for the cover or endorse your book, get it in writing. When you aim at the bull's-eye, you must be on target.

The best news is, while you may be in the hot seat, the editor is also in the same fiery place at the same time. To stay in business, editors *must continually* find good books. And they're *always* in the market to buy.

Finally, edit and proof your writing until you're absolutely positive that every word, phrase, and sentence burns as brightly as your desire to get published. By that time, the manuscript is probably ready to mail.

So, you get fired up about an idea, shine a light on it from a different direction, set an editor aflame with enthusiasm—then start juggling.

Section One: Letter of Proposal

• • •

Book-length nonfiction is very often contracted for before the book is written. This is because the information must be as up to date as possible. Who knows what could change while you wait to hear from the publishers?

For the same reason, multiple submissions for timely books (sending proposals to several editors or agents at the same time) are more acceptable than in the realm of fiction. First rule for sending multiple submissions: You must let the publishers know what you're doing. Second, underline the word timely here. A biography of Nancy Reagan is not timely—unless perhaps it could tie in with her campaign for the presidency. Don't spoil your book's chances by misusing simultaneous submissions.

When submitting an idea for book-length nonfiction, you send a letter of proposal, an introduction, a tentative table of contents, and, sometimes, one chapter. A letter of proposal is different from a query letter in that it contains more detail about the topic and may be longer. The table of contents lists descriptive chapter titles and subheadings that explain the topic, show how the book is arranged, and how fully it's developed. You may wish to add an explanatory phrase to titles and subheadings to make the subject clearer. (These can be omitted in the final table of contents.)

Your first step is to find the slant you want to use for your subject. Proposing a book on the Civil War is unlikely to fire the editor's imagination. Presenting an idea for a book on women balloonists of the Confederacy has more chance for success . . . if it hasn't already been done.

Next, collect the evidence that will convince the editor that your idea is unique, workable, and potentially profitable. You needn't actually do the reading, research, and interviewing at this point, but you must know what information is available. Editors are particularly interested in seeing that you've thought your topic through, that development is logical, and that there is plenty of material to sustain an entire book.

Research how your book is going to fit into the market. On one hand, you want to show that your book is different from anything already published and presently available. On the other hand, you must show that your idea would appeal to an already defined segment of the buying public. For example, diet books generally sell well; they have appeal to a cross-section of readers. However, your diet book must have something to set it apart from the crowd of others on bookstore shelves. This could be new medical research, the backing of a celebrity, or the sanction of an important organization. A trip to the bookstore and a little time with *Books in Print* will help you find market information.

Write the letter of proposal with the intention of selling the editor on the idea, its marketability, and your expertise. The letter is your promotion.

The introduction (sometimes called The Overview), your marketing tool, must show the editor your writing ability and style.

The table of contents ensures the editor that you are a thorough researcher and intend to cover your subject expertly and in depth.

Author's Name and Title (if applicable)
Author's Address
City, State Zip Code
Phone Number

Date

Editor's Name, Title (or agent)
Publishing Company (or Agency)
Address
City, State Zip Code

Dear Editor's (or agent's) Name:

Most authors will begin the letter of proposal for a nonfiction book with a hook, something to catch the editor's eye and interest him or her in the topic immediately. A quote, anecdote, an important statistic, or a bit of little-known information are all good ways to begin. The hook shows a need your book can answer and fill. Use the TITLE in this first paragraph.

Explain the intended audience for the book. Mention other similar books on the market and tell why yours is different. Name your major audience, include actual numbers, if possible, then cite secondary markets that could logically be included.

If there's extensive research involved, touch on what primary sources are available such as records, old letters, interviews, diaries, newspapers, court cases, medical studies, and so forth. Don't bother mentioning secondary sources, such as research books. You aren't committing yourself to using these collateral materials. You're just establishing that there really is a book's worth of data available.

Give an indication of how long the work will be and how long it will take to complete. Tell the editor that you've included an introduction, a detailed table of contents, and one chapter (if you know the editor wants one). Ordinarily, you don't yet have sample chapters to send, just the introduction and table of contents. When sending multiple submissions, say so, and explain why.

Although you should keep most query letters to one page, you have more flexibility with letters of proposal. Write up to four pages, provided every word, every sentence, every scrap of information is vital for the editor to know now. Be ruthless with your editing. Give the topic ample treatment, but don't give in to the temptation to wax poetic. Save that for the book.

Give your credentials next. Describe any special research or pertinent experimentation. If you or someone else has used your 'program' successfully, describe that experience. If your book has the endorsement of respected professionals in your field, include that information. The more expertise you can show, the better your chances of catching the editor's or agent's eye. Briefly outline what you can and will do to support and enhance promotion of the book. If your credentials are especially impressive and your planned support substantial, you may choose to put this paragraph at the beginning of the letter of proposal.

For a timely idea, tied to a once-in-a-blue-moon event or a hot news item, tell the editor you need an answer by a specific date. Indicate that you'll call him at that time, if you haven't already heard from him. Thank the editor, then assure him that you're open to any editorial suggestions he might want to make.

This sample letter is in block form and single spaced. Paragraphs are not indented and are separated by a blank line. Business-letter form is standard in a letter of proposal. Double spacing, with indented paragraphs, is also acceptable, if preferred by the editor. When using the expanded form, send a brief cover letter explaining what your package contains, a cover sheet, then follow the double-spaced example in Section Two, of Part Five, on page 59.

{**Important:** Before sending out a letter of proposal and accompanying materials, write for a publisher's or an agent's nonfiction proposal guidelines. Some editors and agents want to see a shorter query letter first. They may also want the submission in a different form. Some prefer that each section begin on a separate sheet. For instance: Introduction or Overview, Audience, Competition, Author Background, Marketing, and Promotion. Some may want Chapter Abstracts instead of, or in addition to, a Sample Chapter. *Always* send what an editor wants! Have your proposal package finished when you query so you can offer it immediately. However, if the editor answers the query and asks that you subtract or add something more, by all means revise before sending out the proposal. After getting a positive response from a query, be sure to include a cover letter, reminding the editor or agent that the proposal enclosed was requested. I once received instructions to write "Requested" on the front of the envelope.}

A sample letter of proposal follows.

Sincerely,

Author's Name and Professional Title (if applicable)
Daytime Phone Number
E-mail Address

Clea Alexandria
10 Durrell Lane
Sighkee City, Colorado 00000
ClAl@xxx.com
(555) 555-5555

1 February 2001

Jessica Venice, Senior Editor
Merchant Publishing Company
123 Shake St.
Spear, NY 00000

Dear Ms. Venice:

In 2000, 16 percent of third-grade girls were on a diet, an alarming statistic in this age of obsession with youth and good looks. Are we raising a generation of girls destined for the lack of personal esteem now plaguing their mothers? EVERY GIRL'S GREAT is a handbook for eight- to twelve-year-old girls that mixes fun with esteem-building activities.

EVERY GIRL'S GREAT is the first book for girls just beginning to take an interest in clothes, make-up, and dating. At this age, girls need an ego boost. Instead, they are either told to "quit acting like a child" or to "wait until you grow up." EVERY GIRL'S GREAT fills this gap with games, quizzes, and stories that are equally appropriate to classroom, club, or slumber party.

EVERY GIRL'S GREAT will tap a resource never before used in a help-your-child book--girls themselves. Under the supervision of Dr. Muriel Stegman, professor of child psychology at Greater Colorado University, I have been developing the activities with the constant assistance of girls in the target group. Dr. Stegman and I have permission from the National Tomorrow's Women Leaders Clubs and community officials, in all fifty states, Canada, England, and Australia, to continue the work with their young women for that purpose.

We estimate completion of the research within six months and will need an additional two months before delivering the completed manuscript. Because of the tie-in with the International Young Women's Month, two years from this March, we are offering this idea to other publishers, also. The Young Women's Gala has already received considerable publicity, as you know, and so would be the perfect time to have EVERY GIRL'S GREAT available. Dr. Stegman will be a featured speaker during the Gala, and is already confirmed to appear on seven national and international television talk shows during that week.

The completed manuscript will run about 70,000 words (excluding front and back matter) in approximately fifteen chapters. Dr. Stegman has agreed to write a foreword.

In addition to holding a doctorate in elementary education, I have spent ten years as a teacher, troop leader, and mother--in short, a cheerleader for young girls struggling with the difficulties of becoming young women. We hope all girls will use EVERY GIRL'S GREAT--and believe it!

In order to have EVERY GIRL'S GREAT ready for publication, Dr. Stegman and I are hoping to have a firm offer on this project within the next two months. If I haven't heard from you by then, I'll give you a call the week of 15 July. We look forward to hearing from you soon and working with you in any way we can to make EVERY GIRL'S GREAT the greatest.

Sincerely,

Clea Alexandria, Ph.D.
Daytime Phone Number
ClAl@xxx.com

Enclosures: Introduction / Overview
Table of Contents
Chapter One / 'You're Only Young Once'

Clea Alexandria
10 Durrell Lane
Sighkee City, Colorado 00000
(555) 555-5555
ClAl@xxx.com
SSN 000-00-0000

About 70,000 words

EVERY GIRL'S GREAT

by

Clea Alexandria

Proposal

(Introduction and Table of Contents)

INTRODUCTION

An introduction is written by the author. In the introduction for your proposal, you will present a brief overview of the entire book, a concise premise (two or three sentences), then any ideas or information the reader needs to understand before he begins your book. This is not to say that you must write a condensed course on botany to introduce a book on the habits of the Venus flytrap, although a discussion of carnivorous plants might be essential.

Your initial introduction may change as the book evolves. Don't worry about this. Any information that might interrupt the development of your premise in the text, or any information that complements your topic, goes in the introduction. It is placed just before the beginning of the text itself, except where a list of contributors or chronology is used. (For order of front matter, see table of contents, page 130, in Section Two.)

The introduction for the finished manuscript may be as long or as short as you think necessary. Short introductions are sometimes presented as part of the text of Chapter One. (In this case, when you're putting together your complete manuscript, the first chapter section title could be INTRODUCTION. If you have no other chapter section titles, simply center CHAPTER ONE on a line by itself before starting the chapter proper, as you would do for a chapter section title.)

Longer introductions appear as their own section of the front matter. Number the running header with consecutive page numbers. Center the word INTRODUCTION so it is 1 1/4 inches from the top of the page. Return twice (two double spaces) and begin the text. All other pages of the introduction will have the running header 1/2 inch from the top edge, with text beginning 1 1/4 inches from the top of the page.

As pictured here, the introduction included with the completed manuscript and the introduction included with the proposal are formatted the same, except for the difference in page numbering. (Front matter, in the complete manuscript, is numbered with lower-case Roman numerals to include all front-matter materials sent.) As you write the book, feel free to revise or rewrite, as necessary, if new information comes to light.

Anything that will appear before Chapter One, in the finished book, is referred to as "front matter" or "preliminaries." These include: dedication; epigraph; table of contents; list of illustrations; list of tables; foreword; preface; acknowledgments; introduction; list of contributors; and chronology. This is the order in which front matter appears in a bound book. Of course, not all books will have all these elements. Other items (such as quotes and review excerpts) may also be added, as necessary, to make your book more salable and the most useful to the reader.

{A reminder: All front matter in the finished manuscript is numbered consecutively with lower-case Roman numerals. Don't begin renumbering for every section of front matter.}

And finally, even if you make no changes to the proposal introduction, be sure to send another copy of it (and all front and back matter) along with the completed manuscript. This is true of any material duplicated in the two separate submissions.

Clea Alexandria
10 Durrell Lane
Sighkee City, Colorado 00000
(555) 555-5555
ClAl@xxx.com
SS# 000-00-0000

EVERY GIRL'S GREAT

by

Clea Alexandria

TABLE OF CONTENTS

Meet Priddy and Gus

Activity One: "I have a friend who. . . . "

Activity Two: "Hmm. . . . Let me see."

II. FIVE STEPS TO A BRAND NEW OUTLOOK

Hey! I'm Okay!

High Attitude / High Altitude

Open Your Mouth without Mouthing Off

Tiptoes on a Tightrope: A Matter of Balance

Just Do It Now: Action into Reality

Activity Three: Stumbling Blocks

Activity Four: Masquerade

(Continue, in the manner shown, through the last chapter.)

XV. LOOKING AHEAD: THE MATTER OF COLLEGE

To Go or Not to Go: Options and opportunities

What Mother Never Told You: Planning for a career

Peer Pressure: Learning to trust your instincts

Planning Your Future: How to balance family, career, and play

For Further Reading

Index

About the Author

• Table of Contents

The table of contents, for a letter of proposal sent to an editor, has the author's personal information in the upper left corner. Always include your daytime phone number, e-mail address, and Social Security Number.

The title of the book is approximately centered on the page, vertically and horizontally. Follow with the "by" line, then the author's name, as shown on page 121. Drop down two blank double-spaced lines and center the words TABLE OF CONTENTS. Return twice and begin the listings with the front matter you know you're going to have. Continue with the chapters. Conclude with the back matter you're sure will be included. (See pages 128-142 and 147-161 for more information about front and back matter inclusions.)

All pages have a running header 1/2 inch from the top of the page. A KEY WORD from the title continues at the left margin. The author's last name, a hyphen, and the page number go at the right margin. Do not start renumbering the table of contents. Remember: Page numbers for the front matter that accompanies the *completed manuscript* will be done in consecutive lower-case Roman numerals.

Depending on the organization of your material, you may choose to arrange the contents differently from this sample. The most important format objective is to make sure everything looks attractive and readable.

If you compare this tentative table of contents to the sample that accompanies the completed nonfiction manuscript, on pages 130-131, you'll notice a few differences. The tentative contents lists only some of the front and back matter that will eventually appear. What to include in these sections will be decided as the work progresses. Often the editor will have ideas for illustrations, charts, and so on.

The tentative table of contents has no page number references. When sending the complete manuscript, page numbers will refer to *manuscript* pages, where contents items appear.

Descriptive phrases, after chapter titles and subheadings, should clearly show what topics are being discussed and help the editor to better understand the subject. You may elect to keep none, some, or all of these descriptions in the final table of contents.

This sample table of contents, for the proposal, skips from the first page to the last page. Of course, you will include *all* anticipated chapters, headings, subheadings, and descriptions. Do not be concerned if the tentative table of contents changes as the manuscript develops.

It is important to find out whether the editor or agent wants to see a sample chapter(s). Check market guides or send for guidelines on specific requirements. If a publisher's market guide entry is unclear, incomplete, or lacks editors' names and their titles, send for information, visit their web site, or inquire by letter or phone call. Some publishers and agents have very specific proposal requirements. Follow them exactly. Include a sample chapter in your proposal only if you know that the editor wants one.

Section Two: Complete Manuscript Presentation

• • •

The completed nonfiction book manuscript has so many elements, the writer must be very careful to make sure everything has been included in the submission.

There are two types of items to include with your final package; those things that will be published in the printed book, and those things that are for the publisher's records. Naturally, there is some overlap between these two sections.

The items to be published will include all front and back matter (introductions, prefaces, lists of illustrations, chronologies, forewords, appendices, indexes, glossaries, bibliographies, illustrations, and other related material). This section contains a complete list of the front and back matter and the exact order in which items should appear. Of course, the body of the book is also included in the items to be published.

Materials that will not be published, but should be sent (if applicable) with the complete manuscript include: an artwork inventory, copies of release and waiver forms for artwork, and/or photos, copies of permissions for quotes from copyrighted sources, copies of affidavits, and a list of legends and/or captions. Always keep the signed originals of any and *all* permissions, release and waiver forms, and affidavits in your possession and in a safe place. Most publishing contracts hold the author responsible for all of these documents. Protect yourself at all times!

Artwork may be included with the completed manuscript or sent separately (editor's choice). Number and identify pictures and drawings on the back with a grease pencil, and package between two pieces of heavy cardboard. A piece of tissue on top of each photo or drawing prevents marring. The numbered artwork inventory and legends lists correspond to the numbers and other information written on the back of each piece of art. More about artwork and submission protocol on pages 132-133 and 160-161.

Where possible, send usable copies of photos and artwork and keep originals in a safe place in case (or until) they're requested. Before mailing any original artwork, get permission from the editor to send the package by certified mail, insured, signed receipt requested. In any case, always keep usable copies of all artwork included in the book. Always include the artwork inventory and legends in both manuscript and artwork packages.

Send completed manuscripts and other materials in large padded mailers—the bubble mailers are best. If the manuscript is very long and particularly heavy, put it into a manuscript box first, then into the padded mailer. Typing paper boxes are useful for this purpose, if the book isn't over five hundred manuscript pages long. If you use a box, take the extra precaution of addressing the box, also, before putting it into the addressed mailer. Beneath your return address, on the box, add your phone number and the title of the work.

The most important consideration is getting your manuscript to the editor safely, on deadline, and looking neat and professional.

Author's Name
Address
City, State Zip Code

Date

Editor's Name and Title
Publishing Company
Address
City, State Zip Code

Dear Editor's Name:

A cover letter will accompany the completed manuscript of your nonfiction book. It is really little more than a formality intended to let your editor know what's in your package. In addition to front matter, manuscript, back matter, and artwork, be sure to list all other manuscript materials enclosed that will not appear in the printed book. These might include copies of signed and dated permissions and releases, an artwork inventory, a legends list, and/or any other items you feel necessary or that the editor has requested.

By now, you have probably been in contact with your editor a number of times regarding the progress of your manuscript. If appropriate, you may refer to any previous concerns the editor has had and how you fixed them. Otherwise, keep it short and sweet. An example follows.

Sincerely,

Author's Name
Daytime Phone Number
E-mail Address

Clea Alexandria
10 Durrell Lane
Sighkee City, Colorado 00000

14 December 2001

Jessica Venice, Senior Editor
Merchant Publishing Company
123 Shake St.
Spear, NY 00000

Dear Ms. Venice:

I'm happy to report that ATTITUDE IS EVERYTHING is finished and enclosed. As you asked, I've lengthened the preface to include my observations of the exercises in action. You would have been pleased to see the positive responses Dr. Stegman and I received from a group of local teenagers. We spent an additional thirty hours working with the new activities in the book, and I think we all, adults and young people alike, walked away with a greater respect for the opinions of others.

I have fixed Chapter Three according to your suggestions. You were absolutely right about changing the order of the major subheadings; the whole thing reads much more logically now. In addition to the manuscript, lists of permissions, release and waiver forms, and affidavits, along with copies of the completed forms, an artwork inventory, and a legends list are included with this submission.

By the way, I love the new title, ATTITUDE IS EVERYTHING. I was never particularly happy with EVERY GIRL'S GREAT. Thanks!

Looking forward to hearing from you when you've had a chance to read the whole manuscript, and I'll be happy to make any changes you think necessary.

Sincerely,

Clea Alexandria
(555) 555-5555
ClAl@xxx.com

Clea Alexandria
10 Durrell Lane
Sighkee City, Colorado 00000
(555) 555-5555
ClAl@xxx.com
SSN 000-00-0000

About 70,000 words

ATTITUDE IS EVERYTHING

by

Clea Alexandria, Ph.D.

Foreword by Dr. Muriel Stegman, M.D.

Professor of Child Psychology, Upper Colorado University

DEDICATION

To my sister--

Who never complained about doing double duty as a mother to my three girls while this project was in progress.

To my daughters--

Who hardly ever complained about eating cold suppers.

Who found out, the hard way, why you have to sort laundry.

Who learned that string mops come in One-Size-Fits-All.

Who have always wanted me to be a writer anyway.

The dedication is a short tip of the hat to a person, persons, or group who helped the author in some way in the writing of his or her book.

Begin the running header for the front matter with the appropriate lower-case Roman numeral.

Center the word DEDICATION 1 1/4 inches from the top edge of the paper. Arrange the dedication attractively on the page.

If the dedication runs to more than fifteen or twenty lines, the information belongs in ACKNOWLEDGMENTS or PREFACE.

EPIGRAPH

An epigraph is a short quotation,
Usually pertinent to your subject,
You may include if you wish.
Center it attractively on the page,
Without quotation marks.

--Epigraph Author
Quoted Work

ATTITUDE IS EVERYTHING

TABLE OF CONTENTS

Note: Materials that will not appear in the printed book are not listed here.

LIST OF ILLUSTRATIONS

Center the LIST OF ILLUSTRATIONS 1 1/4 inches from the top of the page. Continue the running header, with sequential page numbers in lower-case Roman numerals, 1/2 inch below the top edge of the paper. Return twice (drop two double spaces). Numbers at the left margin refer to numbers marked on the back of each illustration. Place the words Frontispiece (illustration facing the title page of the printed book, if you're using one) and Facing Page on the left. Tab about 1/2 inch to the right of the page number and type the artwork's title. Page numbers here refer to corresponding manuscript pages. The typesetter will determine the page number references in the printed book. You'll check them in the galleys.

If your editor has specific instructions for formatting this, or any other portion of your manuscript submission, by all means, follow his or her suggestions.

The illustration designation is used for diagrams and maps, line drawings in black and white, drawings in color, and photographs.

Remember: All artwork is numbered (1 of #, 2 of #, etc.) on the back and marked with your name, KEY WORD from the book title, chapter number or title, manuscript page, and a *very short* description. Mark TOP on the back, at the upper top edge of each piece.

Photocopies of each piece of art are numbered, marked, and inserted in the proper place in the manuscript. These inserted copies need not be of high quality, but must be neat, clean, and recognizable.

Always credit the artist or photographer in the legend.

LIST OF TABLES

List Tables in the order they appear in the book. Numbers refer to the number written on the back of the actual table. Page numbers listed refer to the corresponding manuscript pages. Chapter numbers may also be noted, if you wish. The caption further designates and describes the table. {Captions are descriptive words placed above the illustration.)

Remember: *All* art (including tables) is numbered in consecutive order, the order it appears in the manuscript. Refer back to the previous page. Notice that even though the Tables are listed on a separate page, they are numbered sequentially, with the Illustrations, corresponding to their order and place in the manuscript. Therefore: 1) a photo, 2) a table, 3) an illustration, 4) a list presented as a table, 5) a photo, and so on.

Photocopies of each table are numbered, marked, and inserted in the proper place in the manuscript. Again, these copies need not be of high quality, but must be neat, clean, and recognizable.

Tables are a part of your artwork package and will be numbered and marked accordingly. (See instructions on page 132 and 160.) They may be of any type you wish to use, such as: graphs; pie charts; bar graphs; linear charts; lists in columns; etc. Tables, along with all other artwork, are listed in the Artwork Inventory in consecutive order.

Table legends (explanatory or descriptive statements placed below a figure or illustration) appear in the Legends list. See page 161. Captions (titles or headlines for a figure or illustration) should be designated as such in the Legend list. Always credit the artist or creator in the legend.

The appearance of any list should be easy to read and neatly spaced. Use double spacing throughout.

Margins remain the same as for all manuscript pages: Running header 1/2 inch from the top of the page, text margins 1 1/4 inches, or larger, all the way around.

FOREWORD

SMOOTH SAILING AHEAD:
TODAY'S YOUNG WOMAN AS CAPTAIN OF HER OWN SHIP

by

Muriel Stegman, M.D., Founder, Adults for Children's Rights

In a foreword of more than four pages, the author's name and title sometimes appear at the beginning. A title may be used if you wish. After the running header, center FOREWORD 1 1/4 inches from the top of the page. Return twice (drop two double spaces) and center the title (if used). The author's name and title appear on the next line, followed by his or her professional affiliation, if appropriate. Use double spacing throughout.

It is possible that, in the original plan for your book, you didn't intend to include a foreword. Even if that's the case, keep your eyes open, during the course of your research and writing, for a respected person willing to write a foreword. This can be an important factor in how well your book sells after publication. More than likely, the editor will be open to the change in your original design. A foreword by an authority in your field, or a celebrity champion of your cause, can increase book sales dramatically.

Number the foreword consecutively with the rest of the front matter using lower-case Roman numerals. Don't be concerned if items included in the final manuscript's front matter don't match what you originally proposed. The substance of the content may have changed, as you've added and deleted material, or you may have added a dedication and epigraph.

No matter. Just make sure everything's included and the page numbering in the completed manuscript is internally consistent.

The last page of the long foreword will look like this page, with the running header and the appropriate page number.

Since the author of the foreword is not the author of the book, it will be necessary to retype the foreword (unless both authors happen to have identical writing equipment). Everything you send to an editor should be neat, consistent, and easy to read, regardless of whether or not the manuscript has been sold.

At the end of the foreword, you may include the city, state, and date, although some publishers will not include it in the book. However, if you include the information in the complete manuscript, there is always the chance that the editor will choose to use it.

Bonita, Colorado

December 2001

PREFACE

A preface is the author's remarks to the readers. It may contain personal information, such as how the author came to be interested in the topic or what relationship he or she had to the person being written about. Or, the author may choose to recognize someone of particular importance to the research done for the book. (The author may include all thanks in the preface, in which case, the acknowledgments are omitted.)

There are no hard and fast rules to dictate what should be included in the preface. Generally, though, the preface contains personal remarks and observations, while the introduction addresses the subject matter being dealt with in the text. The preface is optional, unless the editor requests it.

A useful guideline for the preface and the rest of the front matter (or preliminaries) is that there should be very little overlap. If the foreword and preface both wax poetic about what a great guy Charles Dickens was, the preface is then unnecessary. If the foreword covers all the information that would have been included in the introduction, the introduction is unnecessary. When choosing between two pieces of front matter, always retain the one that will be the best selling and marketing tool. (A biography of Louis L'Amour will be more impressive with a foreword by Tony Hillerman than with an introduction by author Gertrude Jones.)

A preface is not included in the proposal for a nonfiction book for the very reason that it is not much of a selling point, unless the author is so prominent that any editor or reader would recognize his name. (If you fall into this category, you probably don't need to bother writing a proposal.

Just send a query letter. Or better still, have your agent do it for you.) It is also likely that the preface will be one of the last things the author writes, coming after the research is done, the topic has been fully explored, and the persons deserving of thanks have performed their hours of selfless service.

There may also be an editor's preface. As the name implies, this is not the author's responsibility. It will be added by the editor at some point before the book goes to press. It is appropriate to suggest an editor's preface if you wish.

Begin Page One of the preface with the running header, 1/2 inch from the top of the page. The page number will be in lower-case Roman numerals, numbered consecutively with the rest of the front matter. The word PREFACE should be centered 1 1/4 inches from the top of the page. Return twice (drop two double spaces) and begin your text. The header continues on Page Two and all subsequent pages of the preface. Text on Page Two begins 1 1/4 inches from the top of the page. Double space throughout.

The preface is unsigned, unless there's possible confusion over who wrote it, as in an anthology or a collaboration. If you choose to include a place and date, return twice (drop two double spaces) after the text and put that information at the left margin.

Clea Alexandria
Sighkee, Colorado
December 2001

ACKNOWLEDGMENTS

The acknowledgments section is the author's opportunity to thank individuals or organizations that were particularly helpful in researching and writing the book. This may include your spouse, your librarian, your typist, your editor, your agent, or your inside sources. There are no rules governing who should be named in the acknowledgment section. Logic suggests that there are two ways to go. Either name only one or two of the most important persons involved in the project; or, to avoid hurt feelings, name everyone who made any kind of significant contribution.

Acknowledgments should be included as a separate section of the front matter only if appropriate thanks do not appear elsewhere. So, if your book is dedicated, "To everyone who has helped me along the way, with thanks," there would be no need for acknowledgments. If, however, you thank your spouse in the preface and feel that other thanks are necessary, you may include an acknowledgment section. (In this case, you would mention your spouse again, perhaps last.)

Entries may be made in any manner that seems appropriate: alphabetical, in order of importance, people before organizations, and so forth. Each entry may be on a new line, or the listings may be separated by commas. People may be listed by full name, or less formally, by first name. A brief description of the person's contribution may be included.

The acknowledgments should be the last piece of front matter before the introduction. Follow this double-spaced format example.

INTRODUCTION

Anything that will appear before Chapter One in the finished book is referred to as "front matter" or "preliminaries." These include: dedication; epigraph; table of contents; list of illustrations; list of tables; foreword; preface; acknowledgments; introduction; list of contributors; chronology; and anything else requested by the editor.

All front matter is numbered consecutively with lower-case Roman numerals. Don't begin renumbering for each section of front matter.

An introduction is written by the author and placed just before the beginning of the text itself, except where a list of contributors or chronology is used. (See table of contents, page 130, for order of front matter.) In the introduction, you will present any ideas or information the reader needs to understand before he begins your book. As mentioned earlier, a condensed course on botany to introduce a book on habits of the Venus flytrap isn't necessary, but a discussion of carnivorous plants may be useful. So, the introduction contains information that complements your topic, or information that might interrupt development of the premise in the text.

The introduction may be as long or as short as you think necessary. Short introductions are sometimes presented as part of the text of Chapter One, in which case, the first chapter subtitle will be INTRODUCTION. If you have no other chapter-one section titles, simply center CHAPTER ONE on a line by itself before starting the text.

Longer introductions appear as their own section of the front matter. Continue the running header. Center the word INTRODUCTION 1 1/4 inches from the top of the page. Return twice (two double spaces) and begin the text. All subsequent pages of the introduction have the running header, with the text beginning 1 1/4 inches from the top of the page.

Notice that the introduction included with the completed manuscript here, and the introduction included with the proposal (pages 119-120), are similar. You may discover, in the course of completing the book, however, that there is more material that should appear in the final introduction. If this is the case, feel free to revise or rewrite as necessary.

Remember: Even if you make no changes to the introduction, be sure to send another copy of it (and all front and back matter) along with the completed manuscript. This is true of any duplicated material. There may be a time lag of as much as a year or more between sending the proposal and the completed manuscript. Editors should not be expected to keep track of your materials for that long, so take the time to make the completed manuscript presentation truly complete. The easier you make it for your editor, the more likely he or she is to want to work with you on your next project.

LIST OF CONTRIBUTORS

John Doe, Director of Children's Services for the City of New York, author of Children In Limbo.

Brenda Jones, M.D., Doctor of Pediatrics, City Hospital, New York City, New York.

Muriel Stegman, M.D., Doctor of Pediatrics, Professor of Child Psychology, Upper Colorado University, author of Children's Advocacy Systems in America, Today's Changing Adolescent, and Woman and Girl: Growing Up Female in Modern Society.

List the contributors alphabetically by their last names (example above), however, do not reverse the first and last names. You may include a contributor's qualifications, other works, or biographical information as appropriate. Both here and in manuscript text (if included in the text), contributors' works and other selected items should be typed as follows.

Book titles, essays, cycles of poems, and works issued in microfilm are underlined. There are exceptions to this rule (like the Bible and books of the Bible, which won't be italicized in the printed book), so check a style manual, such as *The Chicago Manual of Style* or *Words into Type*.

Underline titles of court cases and names of the parties in the titles.

Titles of songs and short musical selections are in "quotes."

Operas and oratorios are underlined. Musical selections, titled by number or key, should *not* be underlined or set off by "quotation marks."

Underline newspaper, newsletter, journal, and magazine names. Add the word *magazine,* after the name, if necessary for clarity.

Titles of plays, motion pictures, and television series are underlined. Television episode titles (in a television series) are in "quotes."

The names of vessels; airplanes, airships, spacecraft, submarines, and trains, are underlined. Types of planes are *not* underlined.

Taxonomic names of genera, species, varieties, and genus names are underlined.

Remember: Underline indicates that the word or words are to be typeset in *italics* in the printed book. If in doubt, check a manual of style.

CHRONOLOGY

STAGES OF CHILD DEVELOPMENT

Birth to age two	Nonverbal. The child tests her environment using her senses.
Age two to seven	Linguistic. The child links learned concepts to words and experiments with language.
Age seven to twelve	Logical. The child divides her knowledge into categories.
Age twelve to adult	Philosophical. The child develops her own ideas and values.

A chronology lists important dates, events, or stages that pertain to the subject matter of your book.

Center the word CHRONOLOGY, in upper case letters, 1 1/4 inches from the top of the page. Return twice.

Give the list a title. The title used here is: STAGES OF CHILD DEVELOPMENT

List dates, events, or stages at the left margin. Set the appropriate tabs, after your longest entry, and begin explanations.

Double space the listed entries and neatly space the two columns.

Number the pages of the Chronology consecutively with the other front matter, using lower-case Roman numerals in the running header.

ATTITUDE IS EVERYTHING

by

Clea Alexandria

CHAPTER ONE

YOU'RE ONLY YOUNG ONCE

Happiness Now!

Because of the front matter, the chapters need no cover sheet or personal information. The running header begins using Arabic numerals for the page numbers on this first page of Chapter One.

Center the title, "by," and the author's name, each on a line of its own, then drop two double spaces for the chapter number. Center the chapter name and chapter section title, if any, and double space before beginning the text. Do not underline headings. Underlining indicates italics and would have to be removed before the manuscript can be typeset. That means more work for the editor.

Place title and other headings, which precede the text, high enough on Page One, so that there are seven lines of text on the first page.

There is a certain amount of flexibility in page formatting. For example, it is permissible to have margins anywhere from 1 1/4 to 1 1/2 inches. However, 1 1/4 inches is the standard and much preferred by editors. Smaller margins are <u>not</u> acceptable. Never change margin widths mid-manuscript. <u>Never</u> justify the right margin.

The most important format elements are consistency and overall appearance. Any deviation that makes your manuscript look noticeably different from the accepted norm is likely to brand you as unprofessional.

The second page of Chapter One continues the running header, set 1/2 inch below the top of the page. Text begins 1 1/4 inches from the top edge of the paper.

Some important reminders:

1) Always do a final spell check, after the manuscript is finished.

2) Always recheck grammar.

3) Never send copy with strike-throughs, handwritten insertions, or handwritten margin notes.

4) Do not bind the pages of your complete manuscript submission in any way.

5) To get an approximate word count: Count every word on five <u>full</u> manuscript pages, add totals, and divide by five. Multiply your answer by the total number of manuscript pages, then round to the nearest hundred.

CHAPTER TWO

FIVE STEPS TO A BRAND NEW OUTLOOK

Hey! I'm More Than Just OKAY!

The heading, CHAPTER TWO, should be in approximately the same position on this page as the TITLE is on Page One of Chapter One. You should have ten to twelve lines of text on Page One of Chapter Two. Space your heading lines accordingly. Do not use this page when figuring word-count. Margins remain 1 1/4 inches all the way around. Double spacing and the running header continue. Only the left margin is justified.

Unlike some category fiction novels, such as westerns, romance, or science fiction, there is no standard number of pages for chapters in book-length nonfiction. The requirement here is to deal with only one subject within the limits of each chapter and not worry about length.

The last page of the text proper will indicate that this is the end of the book. Begin with the running header as usual. (By this point, you're probably very good at running headers! Or you've figured out how to make your computer repeat the header throughout.) The text still begins 1 1/4 inches from the top of the page.

After the last line of text in the last chapter, drop down two double spaces (return twice) and center THE END. The symbol -30- is acceptable, but mainly used for newspaper writing. To make the last page as attractive as possible, many authors prefer to have at least seven or so lines of text. (Add or remove lines throughout the rest of the chapter to manipulate the length of the last page of text.) This is purely a matter of aesthetics, not a requirement, but a practice followed in deference to editorial preference.

If the text ends near the bottom of the page, it is permissible to have only one double space before typing THE END. However, those words must never invade the bottom margin. Recast and retype the last page until the notation fits. Remember: Do not bind the pages in any way.

Note: Find further instructions for figuring word count on page 84, in Section Four, Book-Length Fiction. Do not use computer-generated word count.

THE END

APPENDIX A

BACK MATTER: AN EXPLANATION

Back matter is the author's responsibility and should be included with the completed manuscript. The only exception to this is the final index. You should, however, include a preliminary index listing with your manuscript. Index page numbers will refer to manuscript pages.

The appendices are the first items of back matter. Give each appendix a number or letter designation and a title. If there will be only one appendix, a number or letter designation is unnecessary; the word APPENDIX and the title are sufficient. The running header continues. Back matter pages are numbered consecutively with the text. Do not start renumbering the back matter.

Center APPENDIX (designation) 1 1/4 inches from the top of the paper. Center the title beneath. Return twice and begin the text.

An appendix may contain any information the author feels is necessary and yet would be intrusive to include as part of the text, endnotes, or footnotes. Present material in any manner most usable by the reader. This could include charts, graphs, reprinted letters, facsimile documents, discursive explanations, or any other appropriate method of presentation.

For maps, graphs, or other artwork in the appendices, try to design and execute the material yourself or with the help of an outside expert such as a graphic artist or computer expert using graphics software. If this isn't possible, your editor can refer you to the person in the publisher's art department who will give you necessary specifications or assistance.

APPENDIX B

ORDER OF BACK MATTER AND MANUSCRIPT MATERIALS

The following is a list of the back matter and manuscript materials (in parentheses) often included in a nonfiction manuscript, and the proper order in which each back-matter item should appear. Remember that back matter, as front matter, is optional and should be included only if it enhances the usefulness, design, and salability of your book. It is also possible to have other forms of back matter, when necessary, appropriate, and/or requested by the editor, such as maps, graphs, charts, and tables.

1. Appendix (or Appendices)
2. Footnotes [1] or
3. Endnotes [1]
4. List of Abbreviations
5. Glossary
6. For Further Reading
7. Bibliography
8. Index
9. About the Author (and a longer bio for the editor)
10. List of Permissions (and copies of signed forms)
11. List of Release and Waivers (and copies of signed forms)
12. List of Affidavits (and copies of notarized forms)
13. Artwork Inventory
14. Legends and Captions
15. Artwork, if not sent under separate cover

FOOTNOTES

Chapter One

1. Footnotes are used in nonfiction to cite source material used. They also allow the author to include remarks and information not included in the body of the text. Always acknowledge a source.

2. Continue the running header. Center FOOTNOTES 1 1/4 inches from the top of the page. Return twice (two double spaces) and center the chapter number or title. Return twice and begin the notes. Indent each entry. Overrun lines should begin at the left margin. Double space throughout. Leave a blank double-spaced line between entries.

Chapter Two

1. Number the footnote references in the text with superscript[1]. Renumber note references, beginning with[1], in each chapter.

2. Do not place footnotes at the bottom of manuscript pages. It is acceptable to place footnotes, for each chapter, at the end of chapter pages rather than with the back matter. The Table of Contents should reflect this.

3. Many excellent references explain the complexities of footnoting. Our concern here is with the physical make-up of the manuscript page.

ENDNOTES

p.7, Ch. 1 1. Before the 1960s, children's rights were rarely considered in decisions made by parents, educators, medical professionals, or jurors.

p. 29, Ch. 2 1. This information comes from the article "Surviving Parenthood," by Brenda Timonds McMullond, which first appeared in Grown Folks magazine, May 1999.

p. 34, Ch. 2 2. An interesting variation on this exercise uses role-playing, letting girls portray boys and boys, girls. This demonstrates societal stereotypes.

Endnotes are less formal than footnotes. They may include sources, author's remarks, or whatever useful information seems appropriate and helpful.

Whether to use endnotes or footnotes will be a decision made by the editor, or by the author and the editor together. Content should be agreed upon by both the author and editor.

Continue the running header. Center ENDNOTES 1 1/4 inches from the top of the page. Return twice. List the manuscript page number and chapter number or name for each endnote at the left margin. Create columns by using appropriate tab settings. List the note number that refers to the superscript number[1] in the text. Tab 1/4 to 1/2 inch and begin the note. Indent to maintain columns. Return twice (two double-spaced lines) between entries.

As with footnotes, endnote references in the text are numbered with superscript Arabic numerals[1]. Begin renumbering in each chapter.

Endnotes may be packaged, within the manuscript, at the end of each chapter, or with the back matter. Author's choice or editor's preference.

Page numbers for endnotes or footnotes, in the printed book, will be determined by the typesetter, then cross-checked, by you, in the page proofs.

ABBREVIATIONS

ACR	Adults for Children's Rights
BCO	Bonita, Colorado
BVDPR	Bonita Valley Department of Parks and Recreation
MS	Muriel Stegman
MS Papers	Muriel Stegman Papers, Colorado Society of Children's Advocates Archives
UCU	Upper Colorado University, Bonita, Colorado
VM	Valerie Mitchell
VMCG	Valerie Mitchell Center for Girls
WPN	Western Psychiatric Newsletter

Continue the running header, numbering the pages in Arabic numerals consecutively with the text and preceding back matter. Put ABBREVIATIONS 1 1/4 inches from the top of the page.

The abbreviations go flush with the left 1 1/4 inch margin and are listed alphabetically by the first letter of the abbreviation. Set tabs appropriately after the longest abbreviation and begin the explanation.

If the explanation requires more than one line, the second line begins directly beneath the preceding line of the explanation. (See MS Papers above.)

Acronyms are never followed by a period, except at the end of a sentence.

Always spell out the full names of the shortened forms at their first usage in the text. Immediately follow the full name by the abbreviated designation. For all commonly used, standard abbreviations, consult a manual of style such as *The Chicago Manual of Style* or *Words into Type.*

Abbreviations of publications should appear in italics in the printed book so should, therefore, be underlined here in the manuscript.

Note: Abbreviation lists are especially useful to the reader in both technical and scientific works, but any book that contains even moderate use of abbreviations should have a list of abbreviations in the back matter.

GLOSSARY

Adolescence:	In humans, the ages of nine to seventeen.
Fortitude:	A force of will and personality that helps a person (here, particularly a young person) face the trials and challenges of life.
Gratitude:	An attitude of thankfulness for one's circumstances. In ATTITUDE IS EVERYTHING, gratitude especially means an appreciation of universal power.
Platitude:	Here, a belief accepted because of habit rather than conviction.

The glossary is a listing of unusual, difficult, foreign, or technical terms found in the text. These words are listed in alphabetical order and defined either by dictionary meaning, contextual usage, or both.

If using dictionary definitions verbatim, you must obtain permission from the copyright holder and give proper credit in the list of permissions. You will probably want to say thank you in the acknowledgments, also.

The running header continues. Number pages consecutively with the text and preceding back matter. GLOSSARY is centered 1 1/4 inches from the top of the page, and the text begins two double spaces below. Set tabs so that definitions are spaced attractively apart from the glossary word and form a second column. Double space throughout.

FOR FURTHER READING

If you're interested in the life of Valerie Mitchell, see Valerie Mitchell: Life of a Crusader by Renee Oglethorp y Peña and Sing a Song of the Cycles by Gerald Nettles Hielborn.

To read more about young women in the cause of liberation, see Hands Across Tomorrow by Olivia Paynne, Standing Proud, Speaking Loud by Azalea Winthrop Kennedy, Young Women United by the Coalition for Teenage Daughters of Farmers, and Never Say Never to a Nineteen-Year-Old by Sydney Brocklehurst.

This section, if included, may have either a list of further reading material or a double-spaced, discursive paragraph (that looks like this one) about additional readings. In either case, include the running header 1/2 inch from the top of the page, and the title, all caps, 1 1/4 inches from the top edge of the paper. If you're using the list format, leave one blank line between each entry. Complete information, such as publisher, date, city of publication, and so forth is sometimes omitted in less formal books.

In either form, you may arrange entries by title, by subject matter, or degree of significance. Above, an example of subject matter arrangement. Bottom line: Make this and all back matter information as useful to the reader as possible.

BIBLIOGRAPHY

Find specifics of bibliography forms in many excellent references. We deal here only with the physical make-up of the manuscript page.

Begin with the running header and the title, BIBLIOGRAPHY, as for all other back matter.

Double space throughout. This always applies to anything that will be edited and typeset.

Begin each entry flush with the left margin. If an entry is too long to fit on one line, the overrun line should be indented approximately 1/2 inch beneath the first line.

Return twice between entries, leaving a double blank line between each.

Lynn, Mary Elizabeth. The Tavera Legacy. New York: St. Martin's Press, Forge imprint, Tor/Forge Books division, 1995.

A bibliography is a complete alphabetical listing of all the author's sources. Generally, the content of a simple bibliography will include the name (Last, First, Middle or middle initial) of the author of the source book, article, bulletin, report, etc., the underlined title of the source material, the location and name of the publisher, the year of publication, and the number of volumes (if applicable). Remember: The author's name is inverted, surname first, as in the last example above.

An annotated bibliography gives all the facts of publication and a critical appraisal of the material. The author and/or editor will determine which form of bibliographical entries would be most useful to the reader.

INDEX

No matter how much wonderful information is contained in the text of a nonfiction book, it is virtually inaccessible to the reader without an extensive general index. Both the preliminary and the final index are the author's responsibility. Index for the manuscript is created by the author and serves as a useful tool for constructing the final index. (Some editors will ask that the author submit only a page, in the proper place in the back matter, that states "Index to come.")

Base the preliminary index on your complete manuscript submission and the page numbers contained therein. The final index will be adjusted after you receive the page proofs of the typeset book and may be constructed (or altered or refined) by the author or by a professional indexer.

Continue the running header. Center INDEX 1 1/4 inches from the top of the page. Return twice. List index items alphabetically. Follow the main heading with a comma if there are no subheadings, a colon if there are subheadings, and a period if there is a See notation. Capitalize main headings unless otherwise instructed. Separate page numbers with a comma. Separate subheadings with colons. There is always a period in the entry before See and See also notations, and such notations are always underlined. Use no period at the end of an entry.

Double space the index. With entries of more than one line, the overrun lines should be indented about 1/2 inch. Return twice to begin a new alphabetic heading (two double spaces between the A items and the B items, etc.). Continue numbering pages consecutively, as for all back matter.

ABOUT THE AUTHOR

This section includes your credentials and personal history. You would definitely include all education or other experience that has enabled you to write this book. Information about how you came to be interested in this topic, perhaps given in the form of an anecdote, could also be included.

If you wish, you may tell briefly about your non-professional self: number of children, ethnic background, upbringing, habits, and where you currently live. These items are completely optional. Unless such personal statistics directly impact your qualifications for writing this particular book, they are most often left out.

The About-the-Author section is not an excuse to add an autobiographical essay to your book. Condense pertinent information into no more than one page. A paragraph or two would be better.

Note: Your editor will want an additional author biography that will be used for publicity, marketing, and promotion purposes by the publisher. This extended bio will contain all the information in the About the Author section, but will also include place of birth; places you've lived; children, grand children, personal interests and skills; hobbies; friends, relatives, celebrities, and experts who will help publicize and promote the book; lists of national, regional, and local media contacts (TV stations, radio stations, newspapers, magazines); local and regional libraries; nearby bookstores; writers' groups; writers' conferences, schools, colleges, universities, or other appropriate institutions, where you might speak, teach, or conduct workshops; and any other organizations with which you are affiliated. You will also be asked to send a good-quality, professionally done, publicity photo. See page 77.

For your own use, you'll want to design a personal publicity bio. This one-page presentation, with photo incorporated, can be sent out to media and others for publicity and promotional purposes. See pages 76, 77, 164.

LIST OF PERMISSIONS

1) Acme Publishing Co., Ltd., New York, for Children in the New World

2) Barebones Books, San Francisco, for Raising Male Children

It is the responsibility of the author to obtain permissions for the use of *all* previously copyrighted and published materials. Use your publisher's standard permission forms or kits or compose your own letters of request. Find copyright holders by writing to the publisher of the work from which you're quoting and asking for the information and permission at the same time. Use a business letter form. Word your letter simply, something like:

> In the spring of 2002, Merchant Publishing will publish my book, Attitude Is Everything. I'm requesting permission, for non-exclusive world rights, to duplicate, in Attitude Is Everything, paragraphs four and five, page 33 (photocopy enclosed), from Children in the New World, published by Acme Publishing, Ltd., © 1998, New York.
>
> If permission is granted, please sign and date this letter on the lines provided below. Also, please write the acknowledgment you wish to appear in my book, and return the letter in the SASE provided. If you have any questions, I'll be happy to answer them.
>
> In the event that you do not control these rights, please tell me how I may contact the copyright holder.

Forms or letters must be signed and dated by the copyright holders.

Include both your list of permissions and copies of the signed and dated forms or letters with your completed manuscript. Number each form or letter to indicate the total number of permissions included (1 of 3, for example). Label and number copies by hand, or type the information at the top of each page (as for a running header). Example below.

ATTITUDE-Permission Alexandria-Page 1 of 3

List the name of the publisher, author, artist, or photographer who's granting the permission, the grantor's city, and the name of the piece to be used. Underline book, magazine, newsletter, bulletin, and report titles. Enclose "article titles" and "unpublished work titles" in quotes.

Keep at least one copy of each signed/dated permission and all the originals in your files or a safety deposit box.

LIST OF RELEASE AND WAIVERS

1) Alfred Apperson, President, Upper Colorado University. Name and description of the UCU Youth Activity Center, Bonita, Colorado.

2) Samuel Beddplat, Photographer. Photo number 17, titled "Square Dancing Isn't Square."

If you're using unpublished, copyrighted* materials, such as: photographs taken by someone else; artwork, graphs, charts, etc. drawn or created by someone else; a real address or place of business; or a real person's name, photo, and/or experience in the book; you must obtain a release and waiver. {And remember to thank them in print!}

A permission allows you to use previously published, copyrighted material. A release and waiver allows you, the author, to copyright material and facts, in your own name, as they are uniquely incorporated in, and only in, the exact form of your own particular work. You will find a standard form on page 79 (it will not be reprinted here), or your editor will supply you with the publisher's own forms.

As with permissions obtained, you should send a list of the releases included in your package, along with copies of the signed and dated forms.

In alphabetical order by surname, include the name of the artist, photographer, or other person giving the release, and a concise description of the material to be used in your book. Package copies after this list.

Write or type a running header, on the copies, to correspond with your list (1 of 2, for example), as you did for the permission forms.

ATTITUDE-Release and Waiver Alexandria-Page 1 of 2

Always keep copies and the signed and dated original documents in your files or safety deposit box.

* Works created after January 1, 1978, are automatically copyrighted. Under federal copyright law, all published and unpublished ". . . original works of authorship fixed in any tangible medium or expression from which they can be perceived, reproduced or otherwise communicated. . . . " are protected. Since 1 January 1978, as amended in 1999, the period of copyright exists, from the time of creation, for a period consisting of the life of the author plus a term of 70 years after the death of the author. For more copyright information, read *The Chicago Manual of Style*.

LIST OF AFFIDAVITS

1) Samantha Burns, J.D. Source of facts on legal divorce procedure in child vs. parent cases.

2) Alissa Davidson, M.D. Source of facts on the psychological effects of verbal abuse on first-born, three- to five-year-old girls in lower-middle income families.

Libel prevention as well as research accuracy are imperative for both writer and publisher. Using information (text, photos, audio, video, etc.) from sources, other than yourself, requires an affidavit. Whether or not the source is confidential, writers must obtain a form from the publisher or write up a document that:

(1) names the person (or reference) who is the sole source of the factual information;
(2) names the person {you} to whom the facts have been supplied;
(3) describes for what purpose the facts will be used {your book};
(4) states, precisely, all the facts revealed to you, the writer; and
(5) assures that the facts cited are, indeed, true and accurate.

Affidavits must be:

(6) in writing;
(7) signed by the researcher;
(8) with the signature of the researcher duly **witnessed by a notary public**; and
(9) dated, reflecting the date of signing and notarization.

An affidavit, permission, or release and waiver does not guarantee that you or your publisher will not be sued. No one can sign away the constitutional right to sue. These signed and dated forms do, however, maximize your protection under the law, since the truth is a complete defense against libel. Keep originals in a safe place!

ATTITUDE-Affidavit Alexandria-Page 1 of 2

Label each photocopy, as shown above, to indicate the total number of affidavit copies enclosed.

Clea Alexandria
10 Durrell Lane
Sighkee City, Colorado 00000
(555) 555-5555 - ClAl@xxx.com
SSN 000-00-0000

ARTWORK INVENTORY

ATTITUDE IS EVERYTHING

1 of 22. The artwork inventory lists, in order, every piece of artwork sent with your book. Include all charts, graphs, photographs, facsimile documents--any material that requires more than simple typesetting.

2 of 22. The artwork inventory list insures that nothing goes astray in the editor's office during the editing process.

3 of 22. Personal information goes in the upper left corner. This is important: The artwork will be separated from your manuscript. When sending separately, include this list with both manuscript and artwork.

4 of 22. The artwork inventory may be single spaced, with a single blank line between entries. When possible, list all artwork on one page. The fewer pages you send, the less likely anything will be lost.

5 of 22. Center ARTWORK INVENTORY, drop one double space, and center the title of your book. The list begins one double space below the title.

6 of 22. Briefly describe each item. Example: Photo Title: Giving Your Best. Match the list to List of Illustrations and/or Tables (see pages 132-33).

7 of 22. Mark each piece of artwork on the back. Include the item number (1 of 22, for example), your name, a shortened book title (KEY WORD), the chapter number and/or chapter title, the manuscript page where art appears, and an identifying description (Map 6, or Figure 3, for example). Write TOP (on the back) near the upper edge of the artwork or photo to indicate correct positioning. Use a soft pencil or grease pencil and a light touch when labeling artwork. Never use a ballpoint pen. Separate each photo or piece of art in your package with tissue or typing paper.

8 of 22. When sending originals of photos and art (not recommended), remember to get permission from your editor to send the manuscript or art package certified, insured, with a signed receipt requested. Be sure to ask your editor which carrier you should use, since some publishers accept no in-person deliveries that require a signature from the receiver.

9 of 22. Package all art with this artwork inventory and the LEGENDS.

Clea Alexandria
10 Durrell Lane
Sighkee City, Colorado 00000
(555) 555-5555 - ClAl@xxx.com
SSN 000-00-0000

LEGENDS

ATTITUDE IS EVERYTHING

1 of 22. Legends are the explanations that will be printed below each piece of artwork. Write descriptions for each illustration, photo, graph, etc.

2 of 22. Double space the list, since it may be edited. Make sure it's clear which legend goes with which piece of art by numbering the Legends to correspond exactly with the numbering on the artwork, Artwork Inventory, List of Illustrations, and/or List of Tables. If the illustration will have a caption (copy that appears above the art) make it obvious which explanation goes where, by identifying the proper copy as either legend or caption.

3 of 22. Even if the legend copy is incorporated into the text, include this list with the manuscript materials and the art (if sent separately).

4 of 22. Do not write legends or captions on the back of the pieces of art or on bits of paper attached to the artwork. Typesetters can't work from copy on art, and again, this may force delays.

5 of 22. Always supply the legend copy on separate sheets. They will go to the art department along with your artwork and artwork inventory.

Section Three: Checklists

• • •

Letter of Proposal Submission •

1. 9x12 manila envelope + mailing label (if desired)
   - Addressed to a specific editor by name and title
   - Return address
   - Sufficient postage
2. 9x12 manila envelope (folded in half)
   - Addressed to you
   - Sufficient postage (paper-clipped to envelope or cover letter)
3. Postcard with postage
   - Addressed to you (for verification of package arrival)
4. Cover letter (if applicable) with postage clipped to it
5. Letter of Proposal
6. Introduction
7. Table of Contents
8. One chapter (if requested)

Complete Manuscript Submission •

1. Padded envelope and/or manuscript box + mailing label (if desired)
   - Addressed to a specific editor by name and title
   - Return address
   - Sufficient postage
2. Mailing label for return (if work is not under contract)
   - Addressed to you
   - Paper-clipped to cover letter
3. Proper postage for return (if work is not under contract)
   - Send international reply coupons (IRCs) to foreign publishers
   - Attach postage to cover letter with a paper clip
4. Postcard with postage (see page 44)
   - Addressed to you (for verification of manuscript arrival)
5. 9x12 cardboard inserts
   - As required for photos and artwork
6. Tissue or typing paper overlay(s)
   - As required for photos and artwork
7. Cover letter (with return postage and mailing label attached)
8. Cover sheet

Front Matter (as required and/or requested)

9. Dedication
10. Epigraph
11. Table of Contents
12. List of Illustrations

Complete Manuscript Submission - *continued*

13. List of Tables
14. Foreword
15. Preface
16. Acknowledgments
17. Introduction
18. List of Contributors
19. Chronology

20. The Chapters

Back Matter (as required or requested)

21. Appendices
22. Footnotes or—
23. Endnotes
24. Abbreviations
25. Glossary
26. For Further Reading
27. Bibliography
28. Index
29. About the Author
30. List of Permissions

Other Enclosures

31. Permission document copies
32. List of Release and Waivers
33. Release and Waiver document copies
34. List of Affidavits
35. Affidavit document copies
36. Artwork Inventory
37. Legends
38. Artwork (photos, drawings, graphs, charts, maps, tables, etc.)

NOTE: From query to full manuscript, Book-Length Nonfiction submissions are seldom, if ever, submitted to Trade publishers by e-mail. For Web publishers, follow their guidelines for saving and transmitting files.

Mary Lynn

Author • Teacher • Publisher • Editor
aka Angel Milan
Mary Elizabeth Lynn

Accomplishments:

- **Simon & Schuster**: *Autumn Harvest, Snow Spirit, Sonatina, SummerSon, Out of Bounds, Sea of Dreams, SugarFire;*
- **Harlequin/Silhouette**: *Knock Anytime; Anna's Child, Danielle's Doll;*
- **St. Martin's Press** (Tor/Forge division): *The Tavera Legacy*, January '94 hardcover February '95 mass-market paperback
- **CompuPress, Inc.**, *Every Page Perfect: A Full-Size Writer's Manual for Manuscript Format and Submission Protocol*, 1987. Required and supplemental text at universities, colleges, and schools. **Lynnx Ink**, 2nd Edition, 1995. **Toad Hall Press**, 3rd Edition, 1997 **Lynnx Ink** 4th Edition, 2001.
- **Co-founder** and past president of the Southwest Writers Workshop (now SouthWest Writers), a 1200+ member nonprofit teaching organization for writers.
- **Founder, Editor-in-Chief, and Vice President** of Sandia Publishing Corporation where she published over a dozen nonfiction books, four on writing, including Lawrence Block's *Telling Lies for Fun & Profit*, Michael Seidman's *From Printout to Published*, and William Buchanan's *Attack of the Midnight Screamer.*
- **Writing teacher** at the University of Oklahoma, University of Texas at El Paso, Oklahoma Writers Federation, Galaxy Writers, New Mexico Romance Writers, Southwest Writers Workshop, Fact & Fiction Workshop, Novel Writing Workshop, Santa Fe Community College, New Mexico Pen Women, and others.

Honors:

- **Phi Theta Kappa** honor society
- **Parris Award** from Southwest Writers Workshop for her contributions toward educating and assisting writers
- **Anna's Child** was listed on Waldenbooks best-seller list

Contact: 6 Burke Loop, Silver City NM 88061 • 505-388-3813 • mary@writerscenter.com

• Glossary •

abbreviations—A section of the back matter of some books that alphabetically lists all the abbreviations used for words and terms in the text. EPP = *Every Page Perfect.*

about the author(s)—That section of a book (usually located in the back matter) that gives biographical and other appropriate information about the person(s) who wrote the book.

acknowledgments—Usually one page in the front matter portion of a book where the author lists and thanks those people or institutions who have helped with the assembly, research, and/or writing of the book.

acronym—A word or designation formed from the first (or first few) letters of several words. EPP: *Every Page Perfect.*

action (or active) verb—Any verb that shows action. *See* passive verbs.

action—When characters are moving or talking, they are considered "in action."

advance—Payment to an author made before a book is published, sometimes before a book is written. The advance is a loan against future royalties and must be paid back from royalty proceeds before royalty payments are made to the author.

affidavit—A signed, dated, and notarized written document, completed form, or letter, wherein the undersigned source guarantees the validity of the facts and; 1) states all the facts gathered for an author by the source, 2) tells where all stated facts were obtained.

agent—A person, institution, or firm empowered to act for another person. Literary agents normally place authors' works with publishers, negotiate literary contracts, and handle advance and royalty payments for a percentage (usually 15%) of authors' income.

all rights—A license to publish a work, bought by a publisher, that prohibits the writer from using or selling the work anywhere else, in any other country, at any time, for the life of the work.

antagonist—The villain. The character, problem, setting, situation, circumstance (or all of these) that opposes the heroine or hero. Moriarty is the antagonist/adversary of Sherlock Holmes.

anthology—A collection of poems or stories by several different authors (usually in a bound book).

appendix—Material, supplemental to the text, found at the end of a book.

art department—That division of a publishing house that oversees and/or creates cover and body art for a book or other publication.

art fact sheet—A form (supplied by some publishers) to be filled out by the author that contains descriptions of characters, scenes, settings, or other information requested by the editor and/or required by the art department for use in creating cover or body art. Sometimes this information is supplied by the author in letter form.

art facts—Descriptive information, sometimes requested by the editor and supplied by the author, which helps the publisher's art department or contract artists design and create cover or body art for a book.

article—Referring to a written work: A short, nonfiction story written for a newspaper, magazine, newsletter, journal, etc.

artwork inventory—The author-prepared list of all artwork being submitted with any completed manuscript. Numbers on the Artwork Inventory correspond to numbers marked on the back of each photo, line drawing, graph, chart, or other illustration. The list is packaged within the back matter material and also with the artwork, itself, when the artwork is sent under separate cover.

artwork—Illustrations, photographs, charts, graphs, line drawings, paintings, etc. Any artistic, photographic, or graphic-type presentation that won't be edited, but will be included in a finished book, article, story, poem, greeting card, filler, etc.

assigns—The person, persons, or entity to whom an owner legally transfers a claim, right, property, etc.

attachment—An object that is attached to a greeting card which is in addition to the written sentiment and the paper stock.

audience—That segment of the book-buying public that will most likely buy a particular genre, category, or type of book on a given subject. *See* market segment.

• • •

back matter—That portion of a book that follows the text and may contain any or all of the following: appendices, footnotes, endnotes, glossary, abbreviations, for further reading, bibliography, index, about the author, and any other items requested by an editor.

back story—A tool, used by some authors, to further deepen a major character and establish logical bases for motivation toward the book goal. Constructed before the actual novel writing begins, a back story contains every apposite event (pertaining to the book) that has influenced or altered the character's life, from birth to the moment the book opens.

bibliography—An annotated or simple back matter list of the reference sources used by an author.

binding—A folder, binder, paper clip, staple, or other device used to hold the pages of a manuscript together. NEVER bind the pages of any book-length manuscript in any way. It is permissible to paper clip the pages of a short article submission, however.

bio—Shorthand for biography

biography—Also called **author background**. A one-page, or longer, account of an author's accomplishments, publishing credits, expertise, education, and/or experience, as any or all of these pertain to the writing of a particular piece of work. Sometimes called a vita, curriculum vitae, or résumé, the bio may contain a publicity photo and any other relevant information. *See* letter of proposal and proposal.

blank line—In a manuscript or book, a line without type, usually signifying a transition of time, change of setting, or change of characters on stage.

body—In a book, all the pages of a book except the cover.

book goal—The goal a character strives for and wishes to obtain during the time span for a particular book.

book line—All books in a particular category and/or publisher's imprint which are written according to specific guidelines for subject, length, character types, number of subplots, etc., and/or fit a unique genre or category.

book-length fiction—A novel.

book-length nonfiction—A book-length true story, such as a biography; or a plan; manual; guide; factual explanation; handbook; or text about a particular subject.

business letter—A letter written in standard business form that discusses the business aspects of a particular work or project.

by-line—Also byline. In a written work: The line on which the word "by" appears, after which word (on the same line or the line below) the author's name or pseudonym is given.

• • •

calendar sheet—A simple, calendar-like device, used by some authors, to help with plotting the logical sequence of major scenes in a novel. Each square, created by drawing vertical and horizontal lines on a sheet of blank paper, represents the time span of one scene (about 4 pages), and is filled in with a few pertinent word reminders. Also called a plot calendar.

caption—Descriptive words typeset *above* an illustration. *See* legend.

category fiction—Book-length fiction that is easily recognizable as a type or particular genre, such as mystery, science fiction, fantasy, romance, etc. Category books are usually written to a publisher's specific guidelines.

chapter abstracts—For a nonfiction book proposal. Chapter-by-chapter synopses or outlines of each chapter to be included in the finished book.

character complexity—The many different aspects of unique and believable character personality, emotion, psychological makeup, physical characteristics, friends, family background, education, experience, vocation, avocation, loves, hates, etc., incorporated into the structure of major characters in a novel.

character sketch—A brief outline of the many and varied aspects of a character, including (but not limited to) name, age, physical description, education, avocation, vocation, family, flaws, moral or ethical faults, vices, strengths, weaknesses, health status, psychological makeup, philosophy, and religious background.

checklists—Found at the end of each Part of the book, EPP checklists are used for double-checking the proper contents of a manuscript submission package and ensuring proper submission protocol.

chronology—That section of the front matter of a book which lists important dates, events, or stages pertaining to the book's subject. A chronology may also be included in an article or used as a sidebar accompanying an article.

cliffhanger—Literally, when the hero, heroine, or another character is left hanging off the edge of a cliff at the end of a chapter, scene, or segment. Any scene, segment, or chapter ending that leaves a character(s) in extreme jeopardy.

climax (final disaster and the immediately-following dilemma, decision, action, and victory by the hero/heroine)—The turning point. The most intense point in a story, usually near the end, when the main character(s) loses (or seems to lose) everything that's absolutely vital to a happy, satisfying life. Hero/Heroine is usually triumphant over the villain. The climax follows the final crisis or "blackest moment."

competition—Those books, already on the market, that are similar to yours. Also: A portion of the letter of proposal or nonfiction book proposal that names and describes all the competing books and explains why your book is different, better, more complete, and/or desperately needed by this specific market segment.

complete manuscript presentation—The package sent to an editor which includes the finished manuscript, all front and back matter (as appropriate), all necessary manuscript materials and artwork, return postage and mailing label, and a verification postcard.

computer-generated graphics—Illustrations created by a computer graphic artist, on a computer, with a computer graphics software program.

confirmation letter—Substitution for a formal contract between editor/publisher and writer. A letter, from writer to editor, verifying a verbal agreement, stating all contractual points understood by the writer, and usually pertaining to (but not limited to) content of the work, deadline, editorial suggestions and/or changes, publication date, and payment, with two lines indicating places for editor signature and date. Send two copies of the letter and a self-addressed, stamped envelope (SASE) for return of the signed and dated letter. Example on page 42.

contact sheet—A sheet of photographic paper on which there are several, small, printed photographic images. Contact sheets can make pose choosing less expensive.

contents—In *Every Page Perfect*: Refers to the Table of Contents of a book.

copyeditor—An editor who edits text for style, punctuation, grammar, content, continuity, and factual accuracy.

©—Symbol meaning copyright and copyright notice.

copyright—Exclusive ownership of the rights to publish, produce, sell, license, or use in any manner, a literary, dramatic, musical, or artistic work. By law, the copyright is in effect from the moment the work is created to the death of the creator plus fifty years, and may be registered with the Copyright Office in Washington DC. *See* pages 2, 18, 46.

copyright holder—The person or company or entity who owns the copyright and the 'bundle' of rights, or a portions thereof, inherent in a copyrighted work.

copyright notice—The declaration of copyright ownership shown on the cover sheet or first page of a manuscript or the copyright page of a printed book with the words, Notice: Copyright by Author's Name, Year; or © by Author's Name, Year. Abbreviated: Copr.

cover art—A painting, drawing, line drawing, graphic, or other art created for use on the cover of a book.

cover artist—An artist who creates cover art for a book.

cover blurbs—Endorsements, reviews, review excerpts, editor's comments, etc., used as a marketing tool, printed on the front and/or back cover of a book.

cover letter—In a manuscript presentation: The letter to the editor that tells the editor what is contained in the manuscript package.

cover sheet—In a manuscript presentation: A page preceding the manuscript itself that gives personal information about the author, manuscript information, and the notice of copyright. Also: The page preceding the synopsis, in a partial manuscript presentation, Also: The page preceding the thumbnail sketches in a novel series presentation. *See* page 80 for one example of a cover sheet.

credentials—A writer's education, experience, and/or expertise in the area of the subject matter of his/her work.

credits—As pertains to a writer: Published stories, articles, poems, books, etc., that can be proved by tear sheets, copies of stories or articles, or bound and printed books.

• • •

deadline—In the writing business: That week, day, hour, when a manuscript, or other materials, must be finished or must arrive on an editor's or agent's desk.

dedication—In the front matter of a book, that page or space set aside for the author's thank-you to the very special person or persons to whom the entire work is dedicated.

denouement—The revelation of the outcome of the final crisis (blackest moment), solution to the final problem, clarification and unraveling of the plot, and tie-up of all remaining character and reader questions in the last chapter of a novel.

• Glossary •

descriptive phrases—Phrases that create verbal pictures using vivid nouns and active verbs.

dialogue—Those words, set in "quotes," which are spoken by characters in a story.

double spacing—Typing text so that there is a full, single-space blank line between lines of type. Manuscripts must always be double spaced. Find examples throughout *Every Page Perfect.*

drawings—Illustrations, usually drawn with pen and black ink on white paper. Sometimes called line drawings or line copy.

• • •

editor—Any person who edits any kind of written copy, film, or video. Also, a person who writes editorials.

editor's preface—A preface for a book written by the book's editor and used instead of, or in addition to, the author's preface.

editorial requirements—Specific requirements for a particular manuscript and stated in publisher's guidelines and/or a letter from the editor.

elite type—For typewriters: A size of type equivalent to 10-point. NEVER use elite-size type for any manuscript submission. *See* pica type.

endnotes—Like footnotes, but less formal, endnotes are documentary or explanatory comments referring to a specific part of the text. Endnotes for a complete manuscript submission (usually book-length nonfiction) are packaged either at the end of each corresponding chapter, with the back matter, or as instructed by the editor.

endorsement—A favorable comment about a work that sanctions its validity, usefulness, or value. Endorsements are usually written by an expert in the field of the subject matter of the book or by a well-known author in the same genre. Also spelled, indorsement.

epigraph—An inscription, motto, or quotation at the beginning of a book and/or the beginning of chapters. Always credit the writer of the epigraph, and if the quote has been previously published, name the publication from which it came.

• • •

fiction—A story that presumably bears no resemblance or similarity to real persons or events.

filing code—A personally designed filing system, used by professional writers, for keeping track of all works submitted for publication by title and/or publisher/publication, and including such information as: date of submission, editor, rights offered, type of submission, revisions, payment amount and schedule, rejection/acceptance, and date of publication.

filler—Copy that fills up the leftover space in a publication. Writers submit filler copy to magazines, newspapers, newsletters, etc., in such categories as: anecdotes; cartoons; facts; short humor; newsbreaks; light verse; gags; tips; helpful hints; poetry; illustrations; photos; and other information suggested in a publication's guidelines.

first-class mail—A service offered by the United States Postal Service (USPS). Send all manuscripts by first-class mail, unless otherwise instructed by an editor or guidelines.

first draft—Unrevised manuscript copy.

first North American serial rights—The first-time, one-time right/license to publish a story, article, or poem in a periodical, which is distributed in both the United States of America and Canada. This, and all rights, are owned by the writer and licensed to a publisher, producer, or other entity for a limited period of time and/or limited number of appearances in print. Exception to the license period: *See* All Rights.

• Glossary •

first person—Use of the pronoun(s) and/or verb form(s) which refers to the speaker or speakers. I saw. We ran. A piece written in the first person stays in the "I" character's viewpoint. First person is used in many detective stories.

first serial rights—The one-time, first-time right to publish a work in any one of the publisher's periodicals (serials). All other rights belong to the writer. Can also be **First Worldwide Serial Rights** and expanded/limited to certain languages and publications.

fitter—The person who decides on a suitable typeface and size, margins and size, and other criteria for the typesetting of a book. These specifications are sometimes calculated and executed by a typesetter or an editor.

folio—Four pages of a book, made by folding a sheet of paper in half to make two leaves.

font—A specific kind, or an assortment of type styles, designs, and faces used in printing on a press or from a computer.

footnotes—Reference or comment about the text. Also, the documenting or explanatory comments referring to a specific part of the text. Footnotes for a manuscript are packaged either at the end of each corresponding chapter, with the back matter, or as instructed by the editor.

for further reading—That section of the back matter where the author lists other books dealing with the same subject as his/her book.

foreword—Introductory remarks, in the front matter of a book, written by someone other than the author.

format—The makeup and/or arrangement of pages for any manuscript including specifics regarding paper size, kind, and color; type style, size, and color; margin size; page numbering; text lines per page; header content and placement; and binding.

fresh angle—A new way to write about an old subject, a modern way to say a seasoned sentiment, a different approach to any topic, premise, or theme.

front matter—In a manuscript: All items preceding the text, optionally including (but not limited to): dedication, epigraph, table of contents, list of illustrations, list of tables, foreword, preface, acknowledgments, introduction, list of contributors, chronology, and any other item suggested or requested by the editor.

• • •

galley proof—Also called galleys. Usually, the final, typeset version of a book. Sometimes called page proofs, proofs, blue lines, and blues. Note: These terms are very often used interchangeably by many editors and writers. *See* page proof.

genre—Book-length works that are easily recognizable as a type or particular genre, such as mystery, mainstream, true crime, etc.

glossary—An alphabetical listing of technical, unusual, or foreign words or terms and their meanings found in the back matter of some books.

greeting card—Usually, a message of regard and an illustration printed on card stock and sold with a blank envelope. Also, a large market for the free-lance writer.

guidelines—Sometimes called tip sheets, these specifications for manuscript content regarding length, character types, plot and subplot prescriptions, etc., are available from many publishers. Consult a market guide for the area in which you're writing.

• • •

headings—On cover sheets and first manuscripts pages, the centered lines of copy that may include: the title; byline; writer's name and pseudonym; chapter number or name; date, time, and place lines; subtitles; and manuscript type (proposal, partial, synopsis, etc.).

halftone—A photoengraving made by photographing an object (such as a photo or shaded drawing) from behind a fine screen. Also called a line shot, screen, or continuous-tone copy. Also spelled half tone and half-tone.

handbooks—Instructional books that are published especially for writers. Some of the subjects addressed are: Markets, manuscript formatting, crime reference, rhyming, grammar, writing texts, computers, and all manner of dictionaries, encyclopedias, and how-to manuals for almost every genre.

hard copy—Referring here to a typed manuscript submitted on paper. *See* soft copy.

header—Sometimes called a running header. In any manuscript: Informational type, running across the top of the page. A header is placed 1/2 inch from the top edge of the paper and contains a KEY word from the title on the left, the author's last name, a hyphen, and the page number on the right.

hero—The male lead. The major or main male character. The male protagonist in a story.

heroine—The female lead. The major or main female character. The female protagonist in a story.

Hewlett Packard LaserJet 4 ML—A type of laser printer used with a computer. Mentioned in EPP on page 9 and page 48.

hook—In writing: An introductory word, phrase, sentence, or paragraph written in such a way as to catch, snare, or "hook" a reader's interest.

• • •

illustration—Any artwork (excluding tables) in a manuscript or book. Illustrations include (but aren't limited to) photographs, line drawings, maps, paintings, computer art or graphics, watercolors, and graphs.

imprint—A trademark or trade name, imprinted on the cover (usually the spine) representing a particular line (possibly one of several) in a publishing house and designed as a distinctive graphic illustration, or text, or graphic and text. Also, a publisher's note, usually on the title page of a book, naming the publisher, date of publication, and the location of the publishing house. Example: Forge is an imprint of St. Martin's Press in its Tor/Forge Books division, under which imprint St. Martin's Press publishes, "Way-out-of-category mainstream fiction," according to Melissa Ann Singer, Senior Editor.

indented block—Format for a business letter wherein the first line of each single-spaced paragraph is indented.

index—An alphabetical list of words, names, subjects, etc., and the page numbers that correspond to the location of information in a book. A part of the back matter of a book.

inscription—Pertaining to the epigraph, a quote, or dedication in a book. Usually brief and informal.

insertions—In a manuscript: Handwritten words, inserted above a line of text, that are meant to take the place of crossed-out words. NEVER send any manuscript submission with insertions of any kind.

introduction—In the front matter, the preliminary section of a book, written by the author or another person, which usually explains or defines the subject matter.

• Glossary •

inure—Take effect. When something, such as the benefits of owning a copyright or license to publish, begins.

italics—Slanted type that looks like *this.* Used in typesetting to distinguish foreign words, thoughts, emphasized words, etc. Words that are to be typeset in italics in the printed book are underlined in a hard-copy manuscript. NEVER use italics in a manuscript unless requested by an editor. (When text is sent on computer disk or electronically, by modem, and will not be re-set, italics may be required. Always ask your editor.)

• • •

KEY word—An identifying word, chosen from the title of a work, that appears in all caps on the left side of the page in the running header on all but the first page of a hard-copy manuscript. When a manuscript is submitted by soft copy (computer disk or modem) the editor may request that the running header be omitted.

• • •

left justified—Text, in a manuscript, that creates a straight line down the left side of the page and a ragged line (as the text wraps naturally) down the right side of the page. Also called ragged right.

legends—The descriptive or explanatory words, phrases, and/or sentences that are typeset below an illustration. *See* caption.

letter of application—A business letter, written to a greeting card company/publisher, that describes a writer's type of work, an idea for a line of cards, and/or offers samples of a writer's work in the field of greeting card writing, etc., then solicits an editor's request for submissions. Similar to a query letter.

letter of proposal—A business letter, written to an agent or a fiction editor, describing a book idea, project, or work in progress, incorporating a brief synopsis, then soliciting the editor's or agent's request for the submission of a partial or complete manuscript presentation. Also: For a book-length nonfiction submission, the Letter of Proposal contains information on book content, audience, competition, author background, marketing, and promotion, and is accompanied by an introduction or overview, a table of contents, and, if requested by an editor or agent, chapter abstracts and/or, one to three chapters. Always send for nonfiction book proposal guidelines. *See* proposal.

letterhead—Stationery that has been preprinted with the sender's name, address, and daytime phone number.

life goal—Pertaining to a character in a story: The most important thing this character has ever wanted and for which he/she constantly strives against any and all odds.

line count—The number of text lines on a full page of text. Standard number of lines in a manuscript is 25 per each full page.

line edit—Initial editing of a manuscript by an editor. If necessary, the editor corrects grammar, spelling, plot and continuity problems, and sentence structure, etc. . . . or ideally, none of these.

list of affidavits—One of the manuscript materials sent with a completed manuscript. A numbered list of all the signed, dated, and notarized affidavit copies included with and following the back matter of a manuscript package.

list of contributors—That section of the front matter of a manuscript or printed book which lists every person or institution who contributed to the compilation and/or writing of a book. Usually found in book-length nonfiction.

list of illustrations—That section of the front matter of a manuscript or printed book that lists every illustration (excluding tables) in a book.

list of permissions—One of the manuscript materials sent with a completed manuscript. A numbered list of all the signed and dated permission copies included with and following the back matter of a manuscript package.

list of release and waivers—One of the manuscript materials sent with a completed manuscript. A numbered list of all the signed and dated release and waiver copies included with and following the back matter of a manuscript package.

list of tables—That section of the front matter of a manuscript or printed book that lists every table in a book. *The Chicago Manual of Style, 14th Edition*, devotes several pages to the form and configuration of tables. *See* tables. *See also:* page 133 in this book.

lower-case Roman numerals—The lower case of standard Roman numerals such as: iii for III (3), or iv for IV (4).

• • •

Macintosh computer—A type of computer, mentioned on pages 9 and 48 of EPP.

mailer—For manuscripts: A large, bubble-type or padded envelope or manuscript box.

main or major character(s)—Heroine, hero, and/or villain. Those characters who are "on stage" most often throughout a novel, story, or article.

main problem/crisis—The most significant obstacle, conflict, or disaster that stands in the way of the main character's success in reaching his or her book goal. *See* book goal.

major events—Every important thing that happens to a major character or alters a major character's journey toward his/her book goal or, in some cases, life goal.

manuscript—Any typed/written submission to an editor. A manuscript might be submitted in hard copy or soft copy. *See* hard copy and/or soft copy.

manuscript materials—Everything sent in a manuscript package that is not included in either the manuscript text or the front and/or back matter.

manuscript pages—All front matter, back matter, and the text.

map—Sometimes sent with manuscript materials, a map can be a published map, an artist's rendition, or an author's drawing of an existing or fictional place. *See* mock blueprint.

margin—Regarding a manuscript: The space surrounding text. Standard margins are 1.25 inches, or larger, all the way around the text on every manuscript page.

margin, left justified—Text, in a manuscript, that creates a straight line down the left side of the page and a ragged line (as the text wraps naturally) down the right side of the page. Also called ragged right.

margin, right ragged—An uneven margin, created on the right side of the page, when text is not justified or right justified.

market lists—In reference to greeting cards: Greeting card publishers' guidelines are sometimes referred to as market lists.

market news—In the publishing industry: Information, found in trade periodicals, trade publications, and organizational newsletters, about trends, such as: Who's buying what, who's moved where, what's hot, and what's not, etc.

market segment—That percentage of the book-buying public that regularly buys, or is estimated likely to buy, a specific kind of book, either on a particular subject or in a distinctive genre or category.

market share—In the publishing industry: That percentage of the book-buying public that regularly buys, or is estimated likely to buy, a particular publisher's book releases on a given subject, in a specific genre, or across the board.

marketing—In EPP: A section of the letter of proposal or any type of nonfiction book proposal that could qualify for the designation of Sales Brochure. Through the use of statistics, this portion of the submission justifies the commercial viability of your product by substantiating the existence of a prevailing market segment. Statistics are available in several sources such as: Standard & Poors, a current Almanac, and others. Ask your local librarian for help in finding pertinent statistics. In other words: Who, or what professional institutions/societies/organizations, etc., will need to buy your book?

mechanical—Pertaining to greeting cards: A greeting card that has moving or moveable parts. Fold-outs and pop-ups are two examples of mechanical greeting cards.

minor characters—Those characters who are "on stage" less often than the major characters in a story. *See* main/major character(s).

mock blueprint—A line drawing of the layout of a particular place, building, or other type of structure, fictitious or real.

multiple submission—A query, proposal, partial, or finished manuscript that is sent out to several different editors or publishers at the same time. *See* Simultaneous Rights.

• • •

narrative—Broadly, a story. More specifically, that part of a story that is not classically written as dialogue or action, such as introspection and description.

New Century Schoolbook font—A computer font used in Macintosh computers. The computer font (typeface) used throughout *Every Page Perfect*.

news release—A short, nonfiction publicity piece about an upcoming event, usually written for a newspaper, newsletter, or bulletin.

nonexclusive right—Any right granted to another that does not guarantee that the grantee will be the only one accorded that right. e.g.: One time rights can be granted to multiple publishers.

nonfiction book or book-length nonfiction manuscript—A factual book-length work.

novel series premise—The underlying dramatic concept, conflict, goal, and/or character goal and motivation that ties a series of novels together.

novel—A book-length work of fiction.

• • •

one-hundred-line screen—A fine meshlike pattern of crossing vertical and horizontal lines ruled onto a piece of optical glass through which an object, photo, or drawing can be reproduced (photoengraved) to create a 100-dot-per-square-inch halftone or line shot. One-hundred-line screen halftones copy well on a photocopy machine.

one-time rights—(also called Simultaneous Rights). This is the nonexclusive right to publish the work one time. While similar to First Serial Rights, it doesn't guarantee that the publisher will be the first to publish the work. *See* nonexclusive right.

ongoing characters—Major characters who appear in all the books in a series of novels, stories, articles, movies, television shows, computer games, or nonfiction books, etc.

• Glossary •

original slant—A piece written from the unique perspective, attitude, or bias of the writer. *See* fresh angle.

outline proposal—A manuscript submission in which the proposed story is outlined, major scene by major scene, chapter by chapter.

outline—A fairly brief summary of a subject or plot. Sometimes called a synopsis, but differing in that chapter numbers and/or chapter titles are referred to, where appropriate, in the copy. An outline can be longer than 'brief,' when an editor or agent specifies an alternate length. *See* synopsis. *See also*, pages 49, 56, 62-63, 71.

over the transom—A term used by editors that refers to a manuscript that has arrived on an editor's desk uninvited, unagented, and/or unsolicited.

overview—In an introduction: A general idea of the subject matter of a nonfiction book and the reasoning behind the plan and structure of the presentation. This is sometimes a separate part of a nonfiction book proposal, depending on a specific editor's or agent's guidelines.

• • •

page number—For manuscripts: Page numbers appear in a running header, on the right side of the page, after the author's last name and a hyphen. *See* header. Number front matter pages with lower-case Roman numerals (i, ii, iii, etc.). Number body and the back matter pages consecutively (1 through #). Manuscript cover sheets are not counted as a page or numbered. See examples and explanations of page numbering rules and standards throughout *Every Page Perfect*.

page proof—The final, unbound, typeset version of a book. Sometimes referred to as galleys or galley proofs. Page proofs are often bound and sent to reviewers. *See* galley proof.

partial manuscript presentation—For a novel, a submission of the first three chapters and a plot synopsis or outline of Chapter One (or Four) through Chapter Last, or specific items requested by an editor. For a book-length nonfiction, usually a submission consisting of a letter of proposal, an introduction, a table of contents, and, if requested by an editor, one to three chapters (not necessarily sequential). Usually called a Letter of Proposal or Proposal for book-length nonfiction.

partial manuscript—For fiction: Several chapters (usually three) and a plot synopsis or outline. *See* partial manuscript presentation, letter of proposal, or proposal.

partial—*See* partial manuscript presentation, letter of proposal, or proposal.

passive verb—Any verb that does not show action. Am, is, are, was, were, be, being, and been are used in passive verb forms.

past tense—Using the past tense of a verb, as in: She walked. Also called the ever-present past tense. *See* present tense.

permission form—A form writers use, sometimes supplied by the publisher (in a kit with instructions), that obtains permission(s) from the copyright holder (owner), to use previously published, copyrighted material. Getting permission to use copyrighted material in a written work is the author's responsibility.

permission—Permission, in writing, from the copyright holder (owner), for use of any previously copyrighted material that an author wants to use in his or her own copyrighted work. Use a publisher's form or write a letter that includes: The request for use; exact wording of the copyrighted work (or excerpt); title and author of the work in which the borrowed words, stanzas, or passages, will be published; name of the publication in which the material was originally published; and both a signature line and a date line (to filled out by the copyright owner). *See* page 157.

photo mailer—An envelope of sturdy construction and/or an envelope containing rigid cardboard inserts and marked, "Photo: Do Not Bend," for mailing photos and artwork. Use when mailing artwork separately from a manuscript.

pica type—A typeface for a typewriter. Pica type is similar to many 12-point computer fonts and measures about 10 characters per inch. When choosing a pica-size type, be sure to select a serif typeface. *See* serif.

pitch—Referring to typewriter typeface size. A 10-pitch typeface is approximately equivalent to a 12-point font (about 10 characters per inch) and usually referred to as Pica. A 12-pitch typewriter typeface is smaller and referred to as Elite type. NEVER use elite type for any manuscript submission.

pitch—A very brief verbal presentation of a story presented to an agent, editor, or a producer of movies or television scripts.

plot—In a novel or short story: The sequence of events through which characters move toward the resolution(s) of the problem(s) that confront them.

plot calendar—*See* calendar sheet.

plot outline—The outline of a plot, major event by major event, written in chronological sequence with about two sentences per scene. Also called Sequence Outline.

plot summary—Usually, plot outlines of about two pages in length that are done for a fiction proposal or query and proposal. In a novel series submission, plot summaries are one page or one or two paragraphs in length and are called Thumbnail Sketches.

point size—Referring to computer font or type size. 12-point type is the optimal size for manuscript preparation. *See* page 48 of the text for exceptions.

popular psychology—A category of book-length nonfiction, usually a how-to or self-help type book in the field of psychology. Also called pop-psyche.

preface—Usually written by the author; preliminary and/or introductory remarks that introduce the subject, plan, and purpose of a book and may contain acknowledgments and thank yous to those who helped with compilation, research, writing, or publishing. A preface is sometimes written by the editor. *See* editor's preface.

preliminaries—Another name for the front matter of a book.

premise—The underlying dramatic concept, conflict, goal, or character motivation that ties together the major events in a plot or the overall subject and plan of a nonfiction book.

present tense—Using the present tense of a verb, as in: She walks.

press kit—A collection of information about an author and a book, usually presented in an attractive folder, including (but not limited to) a book cover, reviews or review excerpts, endorsements, one-page author bio, and publicity photo. Press kits can be made up by the publisher or the author. *See* pages 13 and 76.

professional writer—One who writes (full or part-time) for money and is knowledgeable of professional practices and the manner in which the *business of writing* is conducted.

promotion—Referring to all the publisher's and author's book sales tactics. Specifically, promotional materials used by publisher or author to promote a book such as: bookmarks, pens, wearable buttons or badges, T-shirts, posters, press kits, direct mailings, or any other giveaway objects used to sell books. When referring to a portion of a nonfiction letter of proposal or a separate section of a nonfiction book proposal, promotion regards the specific intentions of an author as to how he/she will support the sales effort for a book.

proposal—For a book: Setting forth an idea, in letter form or format specified by an editor or agent, for the publication of a nonfiction book dealing with a specific subject or a novel written in a specific genre. A proposal contains information on book content, audience, competition, author background, marketing, and promotion, and is accompanied by an introduction or overview, a table of contents, and, if requested by an editor or agent, chapter abstracts and/or, one to three chapters. Always send for nonfiction book proposal guidelines. For an article: Usually a query letter that suggests a short nonfiction piece on a particular subject.

protagonist(s)—The heroine and/or hero of a novel. *See also* antagonist.

protocol—Regarding manuscript submissions: The courtesies and considerations expected and required from professional writers when dealing with those in the publishing industry. Consider *Every Page Perfect* the "document" that reflects the etiquette mutually agreed upon by the parties involved; writer, editor, agent.

pseudonym—A fictitious name, used in a by-line, that is not the legal name of the author of the work. Also called a pen name or *nom de plume* (Fr.). *See* w/a.

publicity photo—A photograph, usually in black and white, used for publicity purposes in the promotion of a book.

publicity—Strictly speaking, any *free* media coverage about a work and/or its author.

publisher's line(s)—Specific categories of books, published by a publishing house, delineated by genre, length, formula, character types, etc. Each separate category is said to be a "line." *See* imprint.

• • •

query and proposal—For fiction: A manuscript presentation that includes a short query/ cover letter that introduces you and your credits/credentials and a proposal in either outline or synopsis form. A query and proposal can also be in the form of a single letter done in business-letter form. Submit only when requested. For nonfiction: A query letter would precede submission of the proposal. *See* letter of proposal and proposal.

query letter submission—A business-type letter wherein the author proposes an idea for a book or an article by describing characters, plot, subject, length, etc., with the express purpose of getting an editor to solicit a manuscript submission. Your credits and credentials are included in the body of the letter.

quote—In EPP: An epigraph. Also a statement, from a knowledgeable person, about the content, style, efficacy, and/or excellence of a literary work.

• • •

release and waiver—A legal document (consent form), signed and dated, used to obtain a license (before publication) to use a real (public or private) person's name or likeness (photo or drawing) or quote (interview) or voice, for either an editorial or a commercial purpose. Editorial releases are sought when your book or article DOES NOT involve a "buy something" message. Celebrity releases, also called 'right of publicity' or model' releases, MUST be obtained when using name, likeness, quote, or voice in a 'product selling' venue. See 'permission form' and 'permission' on page 175.

release form—For greeting card submissions: A publisher's form, filled out, signed, and dated by the writer, stating that the work submitted is original by the author. *See* page 29.

research—For writing: Investigation or inquiry into a subject for the purpose of using the facts gleaned in a literary work. Authors and publishers, from whose work such information is used, must be given credit in the subsequent work, usually in the acknowledgments, preface, bibliography, footnotes, or endnotes. Sources (persons doing research for an author) must submit an affidavit to the author. *See* affidavit.

resolution—That point in a book when the protagonist solves the problem(s) of the plot line of the book. In nonfiction: The assumed or promised result of a course of action (if followed), set down in a book or an article.

résumé—For writers: A one-page or longer account of accomplishments, education, experience, credits, etc., usually tailored for a specific literary work and used for publicity purposes and/or included in a press kit. Sometimes called a bio.

revise/revisions—Referring to manuscript changes required by an editor and made by an author.

rewrite—Recasting sentences, paragraphs, and chapters by changing words, construction, and/or style to make the writing more readable, correct, rhythmic, etc.

rhyming dictionary—A book-length list of rhyming words in alphabetical order, useful to the writer of poetry and verse.

right ragged—*See* margin, right ragged.

rights—Those privileges of license, interest, and ownership in a literary work accorded to an author by copyright law. *See* pages 2, 18, 46.

romantic interest—That "other" person in whom the protagonist has a romantic interest. Also called the romantic lead.

running header—*See* header.

• • •

SAE—Self-addressed envelope.

sans serif—A style of typeface or computer font which has no serif. Like this Helvetica font letter **W**. *See* serif.

SASE—Self-addressed, stamped envelope.

SASP—Self-addressed, stamped postcard.

scene—A self-contained event in a story, with a clear beginning and end, that contains the action and dialogue of the vignette and usually includes a character goal, conflict, disaster, and character's physical reaction.

seasonal material—Work written for a particular publishing/release date and with a specific deadline, such as: Sentiments written for Christmas cards are often submitted from 12 to 18 months ahead of the publication date.

second serial rights—Reprint rights that allow a publication to print a work after it has appeared in print elsewhere. This right is nonexclusive and can be licensed to more than one market. *See* nonexclusive right.

sequence outline—*See* plot outline.

series—A succession of articles, stories, television shows, movies, or books unified by the same premise, characters, or theme. Example: *A is for Alibi* and *B is for Burglar* are two books in Sue Grafton's detective series featuring Kinsey Millhone.

series idea—The recurring, unifying subject, theme, or character(s) that integrates a series of articles, stories, television shows, movies, or books.

series premise—The thematic element common to all articles, stories, television shows, movies, or books in a series.

serif—A small finishing line at the end of the main stroke of a letter, as those at the top of this New Century Schoolbook **W**. Serif typefaces are easier to read than san serif faces.

short nonfiction—An article on a nonfiction subject or about a real person(s) written in the prose style.

short fiction—A short story (often 2000 to 8000 words) about a fictional character, written in the prose style, and usually revolving around one plot problem and its solution.

short story—Short fiction (1,500 to 10,000 words) about a fictional character, written in the prose style, and usually revolving around one plot problem and its solution. A short story of less that 1,500 words is called a short-short or short-short story. Example: See the short short (from 750 words) romantic stories in *Cosmopolitan* magazine.

signed receipt—Suggested mailing option for sending irreplaceable art or valuable manuscript materials. Such packages should also be insured.

simultaneous rights (also called one-time rights)—This is offered when selling work to several publications with circulations that *do not overlap*. A cover letter, explaining what you're doing and why, will be necessary. Make it brief, to the point, and accurate.

slant—The style, approach, or subject of a piece that renders it suitable for a particular publication. Slanting: When a writer constructs a piece in such a way as to target a specific market or reading audience. *See* fresh angle.

slushpile—That stack of unsolicited manuscripts that must wait to be read until the agented and solicited manuscripts are considered.

soft copy—Referring here to a typed manuscript that is submitted on computer disk or sent electronically by modem.

sole proprietor—The single owner of a business. Sole proprietorship: A form of individual ownership of a business used by some writers.

solicited manuscript—A manuscript that has been requested by an editor either in writing or over the phone.

source—First: the book, volume, article, media presentation, etc., which supplies the factual material that will be incorporated into a written work. Second: the person who researches and supplies factual material to an author. *See* affidavit.

stanzas—In a poem: A group of lines, usually tied together with a specific pattern of length, rhythm, and/or rhyme.

statistics—Referring to market statistics such as: Number of books of a specific type, category, or genre sold per year.

story form—A prose narrative, with beginning, middle, and satisfying end, in which a character confronts a problem, struggles with it, solves it, and changes in the process.

strikeover—Here, referring to copy done on a typewriter in which one letter has been typed over another. NEVER submit a manuscript that contains even one strikeover.

• Glossary •

subheadings— In *Every Page Perfect*: A second title or explanatory word, phrase, or sentence, beneath the chapter title or chapter number, that further defines the chapter title or chapter content.

submission protocol—The customary business etiquette governing the manner in which a manuscript is submitted to an editor by a professional writer, including (but not limited to): The writer's use of proper grammar, punctuation, spelling, and manuscript format; adherence to publisher's guidelines; customary sequence of submission; and proper packaging and mailing of manuscript, manuscript materials, and artwork.

synopsis—A condensed but comprehensive version of a novel plot, written in story form and highlighting each *major* scene in chronological order. The synoptic summary introduces the main characters, describes their book goals and motivation toward those goals, explains the major conflicts and disasters the characters face, describes the final disaster, climax, and resolution. The word synopsis is sometimes used interchangeably with the word outline or the term plot outline. *See* book goal and outline.

synopsis proposal—A proposed story idea, written in story form, that solicits an editor to ask for some form of a manuscript, either partial or completed. *See* story form.

• • •

table—A table is usually an array that consists of vertical columns containing figures concerning only one type of information. Money, percentages, statistics, etc., will reside in separate and distinct tables. *The Chicago Manual of Style, 14th Edition*, devotes several pages to the form and configuration of tables.

table of contents—That section of the front matter of a book that lists the chapters, topics, divisions, etc., of a book or manuscript, along with the numbers of the pages on which each may be found.

tension—That suspenseful state of unrelenting anxiety created in a reader when a sympathetic character is unprotected in an indefensible position and faces certain harm or destruction.

tentative table of contents—The table of contents submitted in manuscript form for a book-length nonfiction proposal.

text—All the words, in the body of a book, excluding the front matter, back matter, manuscript materials, and artwork.

THE END—Notation, typed in all caps, at the end of the text of a completed manuscript, at the end of a synopsis, or at the end of an outline for a book. Mark the end of a magazine or newspaper article with either # # #, or -30-.

third person—Referring to a character(s) by using the pronouns he, she, they, etc., as opposed to using the pronoun "I" when writing in the first person.

thumbnail sketch—A very brief synopsis of a story plot, theme, or premise for a book in a series. Thumbnail sketches are one page to one paragraph long and are used to propose ideas for subsequent books in a series of novels.

time span—In EPP: The amount of time that passes between the moment a book begins and the moment when a book is finished.

time-line—A plotting device, used by some writers, that enables them to track plot events in time-for-time, date-by-date, chronological order. A time-line can be constructed in list and/or calendar form. *See* calendar sheet.

title page—The first page of a printed and bound book that states the title of the book, the subtitle (if applicable), the author's name, the publisher, and the place where the book was published. Sometimes confused with the cover sheet for a manuscript. *See* cover sheet.

true crime—Short or book-length nonfiction works about a crime or crimes that really happened and about the real people who committed them. Read Ann Rule's *Stranger Beside Me* for an excellent example of book-length true crime.

twelve-point font—Depending on the design of the typeface, a 12-point computer font generally prints out about 10 characters per inch. *See* page 48.

twenty-five lines per page—The standard number of text lines on a full page of double-spaced manuscript text.

typeface—Referring to metal type blocks or spheres and letters for a typewriter: The top surface of the letter and its artistic design or style. Sometimes used interchangeably with the word font.

typeset—Strictly, text set in type, but usually referring to the printed pages of a book, magazine, newspaper, etc.

typesetter—A person who sets type.

• • •

underline—In a manuscript: The method used to indicate those words the writer wants typeset in italics in the printed book. *See* italics.

unsolicited submission or manuscript—A manuscript sent to an editor or agent which has not been requested by the editor or agent. *See* over the transom.

• • •

valuable consideration—In a contract: That inducement that motivates a party to enter into a contract. This impelling influence need not be money. Example: A photographer may sign a release and waiver to allow an author to use a photograph in exchange for a photo credit in the author's published work.

verification postcard—A self-addressed, stamped postcard (SASP), often included in a manuscript package, that will be returned by the editor when the package is opened. Postcards may be typed or handwritten. Example on page 44.

verse—Any writing stylized by the use of line units of regular length whether poetic, prose, rhyming, or free.

vita—*See* biography.

vivid nouns—Nouns which create a picture in a reader's mind. "Man" is a noun. "Cowboy" is a vivid noun.

• • •

w/a—Notation meaning "writing as" which is placed before a fictitious name to indicate the use of a pseudonym.

word count—The approximate number of words contained in a manuscript. To determine word count, count every word on five full pages of text. Divide this number by 5 to get the approximate number of words per full page. Multiply this words-per-page number by the total number of pages in the manuscript. Do not use computer-generated word count.

word processor—A type of computer, similar to a typewriter, but with features that allow a writer to edit, rewrite, and proof copy on a display screen before printing text on paper. Some word processors contain software that enables writers to check spelling, grammar, and type special letters and punctuation such as these "e's" in résumé.

• Glossary •

working title—A temporary title for a work. If you're not satisfied with a title, place the words "working title" beneath the temporary title on both the cover sheet and page one of chapter one. This alerts the editor so that both the editor and writer can be thinking about a better title.

writers' conference—Typically: An organized gathering of writers, editors, and agents, usually held for the purpose of networking with professionals; pitching story ideas; learning more about the craft of writing, useful techniques, and essential skills; discovering viable markets; and understanding the business of writing. Check trade publications for lists of organizations and conferences.

• • •
• • • •
• • • • •

REMINDER: Write for information about **Lynnx Ink Fact & Fiction Workshops** to: Lynnx Ink, 6 Burke Loop, Silver City NM 88061. E-mail to: <mary@writerscenter.com>. Contact us through our web site <www.writerscenter.com> Or call Monday through Friday, 10 AM to 4 PM MST, 505-388-3813. Fact & Fiction Workshops are conducted by invitation only. Schools, colleges, universities, and writers' groups may contact Lynnx Ink for more information and/or for scheduling future classes for one-, two-, or three-day workshops on the craft and business of writing. Workshop information is available year-round. •

• Index •

• Index •

• Index •

• • •

Colophon

• • •

Cover design by Ted and Mary Lynn. Body design by Mary Lynn.

Cover constructed in QuarkXPress 4.1 on a Power Macintosh G4 and using display fonts **Textile**, Klang MT, and *Script MT Bold*. CMYK color.

Body copy typeset in Microsoft Word 98 and QuarkXPress 4.1 using the New Century Schoolbook font.

Camera-ready body copy printed on a LexMark Optra E310.

Printed in the U.S.A.

A publication from:

Lynnx Ink
6 Burke Loop
Silver City NM 88061
505-388-3813
mary@writerscenter.com
www.writerscenter.com

NOTE: A Colophon gives book production and publication details that may be of interest, especially to those authors who will typeset their own books for self-publishing, on-demand printing, or a small, private publisher.

Order Form - FREE Shipping

Every Page Perfect 4th Edition

• • •

Feel free to make copies of this form.
Please print clearly when filling in the information below.

Name: ______________________________

Address: ______________________________

City: ______________________________

State: ____________________ ZIP: ____________

Phone: ______________________________

E-Mail: ______________________________

Ordering a copy of ***Every Page Perfect*** gives you the opportunity to e-mail your writing questions to Mary Lynn. If she doesn't know the answers, she'll find out.

Check your choices—

❍ I want to be on the 'Ask Mary Lynn' e-mail roster <mary@writerscenter.com>
Or contact Mary through <www.writerscenter.com>

❍ I want to order ***Every Page Perfect***.

❍ Autographed.

Shipping and Handling: ~~$4.00 for one book~~ - **FREE**
~~$1.50 for each additional book to the same address~~

New Mexico Residents: Please add New Mexico State sales tax @ 6.375% for total book cost

➤ Send this form & check or money order to:

➤ **Lynnx Ink**
6 Burke Loop
Silver City NM 88061

EPP $19.95 ea.	$ ________
Additional book	$ ________
Additional book	$ ________
Additional book	$ ________
Sub-total	$ ________
NM State Tax 6.375% ($1.28 ea.)	$ ________
~~S&H $4 +~~ ...	$ **FREE**
TOTAL	$ ________

"What every professional writer should know— and most of us don't."

**• Tony Hillerman
Best-selling Author**